Chilt Teashop Walks

C000066778

Jean Patefield

COUNTRYSIDE BOOKS
NEWBURY BERKSHIRE

COUNTRYSIDE BOOKS
3 Catherine Road
Newbury, Berkshire

To view our complete range of books,
please visit us at
www.contrysidebooks.co.uk

ISBN 1 85306 843 8

Designed by Graham Whiteman
Cover illustration by Colin Doggett
Photographs by the author

Produced through MRM Associates Ltd., Reading
Printed by J. W. Arrowsmith Ltd., Bristol

Contents

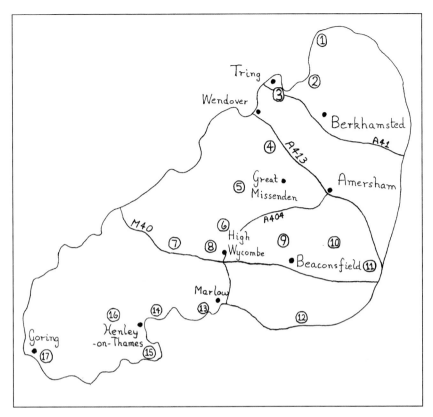

Area map showing the locations of the walks

Key to Sketch Maps

Path on route	— → — —	Teashop	☕
Path not on route	. . .	Pub referred to in text	PH
Road	═══	Point in text	⑤
Major river or canal	〰️	Car park	▢
Stream	∿∿∿	Building or feature referred to in text	▪
Lake or pond	⌇		
Summit	▵	Railway	++++●++++
Church	†		

Introduction

The Chilterns are a range of chalk hills stretching in an arc about 40 miles north and west of London. This description is accurate but conveys nothing of the paradise they are for walkers. Within the 400 square miles encompassed by the Chilterns are about 1,500 miles of public footpaths, mostly quiet, well signed, and lovingly maintained.

The hills are not very high, about 800 feet at most, but nowhere else can such magnificent views be had for so little effort. The Chilterns are essentially made of chalk; indeed the word Chiltern comes from the Saxon word for chalk. This is the cause of so many of the features typical of the Chilterns. Chalk is a very porous rock, and water drains through it rapidly. Therefore the Chilterns are very dry, with little running water. The rivers that do exist such as the Misbourne (walk 4) are small, pathetic things compared with rivers in areas of less permeable geology. However, the walker in the Chilterns is not totally deprived of river scenery, since the southern boundary is one of England's great rivers, the Thames (walks 13, 14, 15 and 17). Much of the charm of the Chiltern landscape comes from the valleys, nearly all dry and locally called bottoms (walks 7 and 11).

If the Chilterns were just chalk, they would resemble the other areas of chalk upland in southern England. However, the tops of the Chilterns are overlaid in many places with clay, which typically forms an impermeable layer and supports quite different flora and fauna. This gives the Chilterns the great variety that contributes so much to their interest and appeal.

The glory of the Chilterns is undoubtedly the beech woods, for which they are famous: majestic without leaves in winter; carpeted with bluebells in spring; luminous green in summer; and brilliantly aflame in autumn. The woods are not composed solely of beech, of course. Oak is common along with many other species.

The beech woods are so dominant in the Chilterns as a result of the demands of the furniture industry centred in High Wycombe. By the 17th century, the woodlands in much of southern England had been cleared, but the Chilterns were still heavily wooded. They became important as a source of firewood for London and large amounts were sent by river through ports like Henley (walk 14) and Marlow (walk 13). At the time when coal was replacing wood as a fuel, the furniture industry grew in importance, and so the demand for wood continued.

It is the landscape of the Chilterns, designated an Area of Outstanding Natural Beauty, which attracts the walker, but throughout the area are market towns and villages of great antiquity and interest. Many of the villages, such as Aldbury (walk 2), West Wycombe (walk 8), and Hambleden (walk 14), are gems of English vernacular architecture in perfect settings, while many of the market and coaching towns, such as Wendover (walk 4) and Tring (walk 3), have a great sense of place and are fascinating to explore. Teashops are often found in towns and villages, and so most of the walks described in this book visit an interesting old town or village.

Situated so conveniently between London and Oxford, the district has been favoured by both church and state. There are many great estates, such as Ashridge (walk 1), West Wycombe (walk 8), and Greys Court (walk 16), and up to the Dissolution monasteries abounded (walks 1 and 4). Despite this, the Chilterns were well known as a hotbed of dissent and defiance of authority. Chiltern people were prominent in the Lollard rising of 1413–14, and later, in the 16th century, dissenters were burned at the stake in Amersham. The Quakers, often imprisoned for their refusal to accept the established church, also flourished in the Chilterns (walk 11).

Tea is often said to be the best meal to eat out in England, and I believe tea is a meal to be enjoyed on all possible occasions. Scones with clotted cream and strawberry jam, delicious home-made cakes; toasted teacakes dripping with butter in winter; delicate cucumber sandwiches in summer, all washed down with the cup that cheers: these are some of the best, typically English food available, and often excellent value. Bad for the figure maybe, but the walking will see to that.

The best teashops serve a range of cakes, including fruitcake, all home-made, as well as scones and other temptations. Teapots should be capacious and pour properly. Many of the teashops visited on these walks fulfil all these criteria admirably, and they all offer a good cup of tea. They always have at least light lunches available as well; so there is no need to think of these walks as just something for the afternoons.

However, the Chilterns for all their beauty and accessibility, are not a well-known tourist area, and there are not as many traditional teashops as in some other areas. Indeed, there are fewer than there were even ten years ago, owing to the very high cost of property in this favoured corner of England and the effects of business rates. Therefore several of the teashops visited on the walks in this book are run in conjunction with other enterprises such as garden centres and stately homes. These tend to be excellent value for money, as the costs are subsumed into the overall costs of the business. However, all the establishments suggested offer a good tea part way round an attractive walk.

The opening times and telephone number of each teashop are given. Some are rather vague about when they open out of season; it seems to depend on weather and mood. If you are planning a walk on a wet November Tuesday, for example, a call to check that tea will actually be available that day is a wise precaution. A few are definitely closed in the depths of winter, and for these walks, where possible, an alternative source of refreshment is given. In most cases, these are pubs serving food, which in some cases includes tea.

The delights of summer walking are obvious. Many of the teashops featured in this book have an attractive garden where tea can be taken outside when the weather is suitable. However, let me urge you not to overlook the pleasures of a good walk in winter. The roads and paths are quieter, and what could be better than sitting by an open fire in a cosy teashop scoffing crumpets that you can enjoy with a clear conscience, due to the brisk walk to get them! But a word of warning about winter walks in the Chilterns. In some places after rain the mud can be ferocious and it is particularly bad on any path that is also a bridleway and churned up by horses. Where an alternative path is available, it is suggested. At such times, wellies or boots are very welcome. At other times fairly stout shoes are all that is required.

The 17 walks in this book explore the varied landscapes of the Chilterns. They are all between four and seven miles long and should be well within the capacity of the average person, including those of mature years and families with children. They are intended to take the walker through this attractive corner of England at a gentle pace, with plenty of time to stop and stare, to savour the beauty and interest all around. A dedicated yomper and stomper could probably knock off the whole book in a single weekend, but in doing so they would have missed the point and seen nothing. To fully appreciate the countryside, it is necessary to go slowly with your eyes and ears open. All the walks are circular with one exception: the walk between Great Missenden and Wendover is an exhilarating ridge walk and uses the frequent train service to return to the starting point.

Some of the walks are short and level, ideal for a pipe opener on a winter's day or giving plenty of time to dawdle away a summer's afternoon. Others are longer or more strenuous, some making an excellent all-day expedition. Certain walks involve some climbing; this is inevitable, as hills add enormous interest to the countryside and with no hills there are no views. However, this presents no problem to the sensible walker who has three uphill gears – slowly, very slowly, and admiring the view.

All the routes are on public rights of way or permissive paths and have been carefully checked, but, of course, in the countryside things do change: a stile replaces a gate, or a wood is extended. In the Chilterns the footpaths are guarded by the Chiltern Society and nearly always marked by white or occasionally yellow or blue arrows. In certain areas where there is unrestricted public access, such as Ashridge or Naphill Common, there are many other, unmarked paths, and careful attention should be paid to the directions. A sketch map illustrates each walk with the point numbers cross-referenced to the directions. An Ordnance Survey map is useful as well, especially for identifying the main features of views. The Explorer 1:25,000 (2½ inches to 1 mile) series is by far the best to use for walking. Sheets 171 Chiltern Hills West, Henley-on-Thames & Wallingford; 172 Chiltern Hills East, High Wycombe, Maidenhead; and 181 Chiltern Hills North, Aylesbury, Berkhamsted cover the walks in this book. The grid reference of the starting point and the appropriate map are given for each walk.

The walks are designed so that, having started where suggested, the teashop is reached in the second half, thus a really good appetite for tea can be worked up and then its effects walked off. Some walks start at a car park, which is ideal. Where this is not possible, the suggested starting place will always have somewhere where a few cars can be left without endangering other traffic or causing inconvenience. However, it sometimes fits in better with the plans for the day to start and finish at the teashop and so for each walk there are details of how to do this.

So, put on your walking shoes and prepare to be delighted by the charms of the Chilterns and refreshed by a traditional English tea!

Jean Patefield

9

Walk 1
IVINGHOE BEACON AND ASHRIDGE

This is an exceptional Chilterns walk with the best of everything that makes this area such a pleasure to explore on foot. Much of it is within the Ashridge estate, now owned by the National Trust. There are woodlands, commons, and chalk downland supporting a rich variety of wildlife and offering a splendid route through outstanding scenery. There are commanding views from Ivinghoe Beacon, with vistas stretching for miles. The focal point of the area is the monument, erected in 1832, to the Duke of Bridgewater, which overlooks an excellent National Trust teashop.

The Monument Café offers an excellent choice of delicious cakes and other teatime treats, and tea in capacious mugs. Also served are light lunches of sandwiches and baguettes, with soup and daily specials such as quiche and salad. Most of the tables are outside in this lovely setting, some under cover, and there are a few tables indoors. They are open until 5 pm every day, from noon at the weekend and from 1 pm during the week, from late March until mid-December. Telephone: 01442 851227.

DISTANCE: 7 miles.
MAP: OS Explorer 181 Chiltern Hills North, Aylesbury.
STARTING POINT: Car park near Ringshall (GR 981142).
HOW TO GET THERE: From the B4506, Berkhamsted–Dagnall road, about 5 miles north of Berkhamsted at Ringshall, take Beacon Road for about 350 yards to a track on the left. This leads to an informal car park after about 150 yards.
ALTERNATIVE STARTING POINT: If you wish to visit the teashop at the beginning or end of your walk, start in the main Ashridge car park. The teashop is next to the visitor centre. You will then start the walk at point 9.

THE WALK

1. Return along the track to the road and turn right for 50 yards. Turn left on a signed path along a track. When the track ends at the entrance to Ringshall reservoir, continue ahead to the right of the fence.

2. At the end of the fence, turn left to a stile and then carry on along the right-hand side of three fields, walking with a wood on the right. Now keep ahead across the next two fields, heading towards a farm.

3. Turn left, then right, then right again, to follow a waymarked path between farm buildings. At the end of the farmyard, turn left on a path, shortly to reach a stile into a wood, and follow the path steeply downhill. At the bottom join a larger path coming in from the left and continue through the wood. When the path forks, bear left, as indicated by waymarks on a post, and press ahead out of the wood.

4. Some 30 yards after leaving the wood, bear right at a fork to reach a kissing gate by a field gate. Through the gate, follow the clear path along the right-hand side of a field, then on across the field, and along the right-hand side of a second field.

5. Turn left uphill along a track. At the top of a rise, turn left off the track and follow the path up to the trig point on Ivinghoe Beacon.

The views from this point are outstanding and include a white lion carved into the hillside above Whipsnade Zoo. Ivinghoe Beacon is the start of the Ridgeway

11

(see walk 3, page 22). The hill supports a mix of chalk grassland and scrub. This is a man-made landscape, the consequence of grazing by rabbits and sheep, and without the nibbling animals it would quickly revert to scrub and then woods. The animals' teeth nip off any tender, germinating trees or shrubs and prevent them becoming established. Nationally, there has been a substantial decline in chalk grassland in recent decades. Much has been ploughed up on gentler gradients. On steeper slopes, the threat is from the changed economics of farming, which make sheep rearing less attractive, and smaller rabbit populations as a result of myxomatosis. Management, in the form of controlled grazing and weeding out of scrub, is essential and here aims to maintain a mosaic of habitats to support as diverse a range of species as possible.

6. Turn left and follow the path down to a road, avoiding a left fork to a car park. Cross the road and continue ahead on the main track, first uphill, and then contouring round the hillside to eventually reach a T-junction with a major track.

7. Turn right.

The Ashridge Estate came into the hands of the Egerton family in 1604 and there it remained until 1921, when the will of the final private owner decreed it was to be sold. Until then, people in the area had enjoyed the freedom of this beautiful area, but that soon changed as the trustees set about disposing of the estate piecemeal. Many mature trees were felled and sold for timber. Fortunately, some influential people were appalled. The prominent historian Professor G.M. Trevelyan approached the National Trust. At the same time Miss Bridget Talbot, a cousin of the Egerton family, approached the Prime Minister, Stanley Baldwin. He, together with the leaders of the other two parties and the National Trust, appealed to the public to raise the money, and to the trustees for time. These petitions brought an outstanding response, especially among local people, and enabled the National Trust to buy 1,700 acres immediately and other parcels of land at intervals since.

8. When the track forks after just under ½ mile, bear left. This shortly becomes a path, after a gate by a house. Follow this delightful path to the Bridgewater Monument, and then for a short distance to the teashop.

In 1748, at the age of 11, Francis Egerton became the third Duke of Bridgewater. He grew up to be a man of enormous body and not a little eccentricity. He

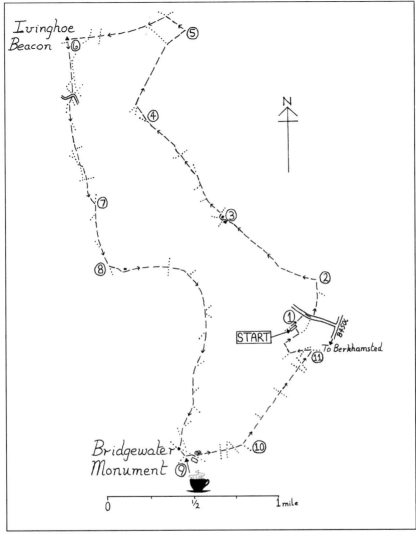

swore he would never again speak to a woman after his fiancée broke off their engagement and he kept his word, as far as is known. His fame today rests on his collaboration with an illiterate but inspired engineer called James Brindley. One supplied the cash and the other the know-how to build the first entirely artificial canal in Britain. Its purpose was to carry coal from the duke's mines at Worsley into Manchester. It cut the price of coal in the city by half and inspired a transport revolution. A later Francis Egerton left £13,500 for a

The Bridgewater monument has 172 steps

monument to be built to his own design, commemorating his illustrious ancestor. Lady Bridgewater thought the design in poor taste and had it built well away from the house. It is 108 feet high and has 172 steps. It is open at the weekend in the summer, and, if you have stamina for the climb, you will be rewarded with magnificent views of the surrounding countryside.

9. Turn right out of the teashop to walk along the main drive. Almost immediately, bear left off the drive to pick up a woodland path to the right of a small pond. Go forward along this path over three cross paths to a fork.

Ashridge House, which can be glimpsed through the trees along the entrance drive, is the latest of several buildings on the site. Richard, Earl of Cornwall, Henry III's brother, brought a golden box containing what was said to be the blood of Christ back from the crusades. In 1276 Richard's son Edmund founded a monastery here, which was a site of pilgrimage and received many rich offerings. It is said to have been connected to a nearby nunnery by a secret passage, but perhaps that is just Dissolution gossip! In 1539 Henry VIII closed the monastery and showed the relic to be a fake. The place became a home for his children, and the future Elizabeth I was staying there in 1554 when she was arrested on suspicion of being involved in a plot to remove Mary from the throne. The present building was started at the beginning of the 19th century and took ten years to complete. It was designed by James Wyatt, known as 'The Destroyer' for his works on various English cathedrals. Views on the house vary: some have considered it a monstrosity, while others have called it spectacular, but it is certainly a classic example of Gothic revival. The National Trust does not own it and today it is a well-known management college, open to the public on a few days each year.

10. Bear left. Follow this path for a good ½ mile until it ends at a T-junction with a cross path.

11. Turn left. Follow the main path more or less ahead at a junction after 100 yards. After a further 200 yards, turn right along a grassy ride and follow it round to the right after 175 yards and back to the car park where the walk started.

Walk 2
THE GRAND UNION CANAL
AND ALDBURY

Aldbury is the quintessential picture postcard village, with many attractive buildings grouped around the village green, complete with pond and ducks. It nestles in a fold in the Chiltern escarpment, not far from where the Grand Union Canal traverses the hills at the Tring Gap. This charming walk links these two features, starting with an easy stretch by the canal.

One of the old buildings in the centre of the village houses a traditional farmhouse tearoom. Town Farm Tea Room is in a lovely setting, and there are seats outside in the garden. It offers a range of teas, including a farmhouse tea with a boiled egg! The cream tea features excellent scones. For lunch there is a choice of sandwiches or a ploughman's. The teashop is open every day except Christmas Day, between 10 am and 5.30 pm. Telephone: 01442 851239.

DISTANCE: 5 miles.

MAP: OS Explorer 181 Chiltern Hills North, Aylesbury.

STARTING POINT: Parking area at the junction of Station Road and Beggars Lane, near Tring Station (GR 947121). If this is full, use the car park at Tring station (charge on weekdays).

HOW TO GET THERE: Tring station is not in Tring town but about 2 miles east. It is signed from the A4251 and from the town.

ALTERNATIVE STARTING POINT: If you wish to visit the teashop at the beginning or end of your walk, start in Aldbury, where there is ample parking in the village car park, passed at point 9 and signed from the village centre. There is also some more limited parking in the middle of the village. The teashop is across the road from the village pub, the Greyhound. You will then start the walk at point 9.

THE WALK

1. Return to the junction of Station Road and Beggars Lane. Turn right over the canal and go down some steps on the left to the canal towpath. Turn left for about 1½ miles to the second bridge, number 137, at Cow Roast Lock.

The Grand Union canal is a great feat of Victorian engineering. It passes through Tring Gap, which has always been a natural route through the Chilterns and so attracted monumental engineering works from the Romans onwards. The canal was originally called the Grand Junction Canal and was part of a scheme to link the Trent with the Thames, so that coal and other cargoes could be transported economically to London from the Midlands and the North. It was built by William Jessop, who constructed a series of locks to take boats up and over the Chilterns. Every time lock gates are opened some water is lost, and in the dry Chilterns there is no natural source for replenishment. The solution was to build a number of reservoirs near Tring, from which water could be pumped up into the canal. These are now nature reserves, famous for the variety of bird life they attract. Cow Roast Lock is not, as might be imagined, the site of some gigantic barbecue, but is a corruption of the term cow rest. This was a favourite resting place of drovers as they took cattle through the hills to the London markets.

2. Turn left along the lane for 200 yards, and then cross a stile on the left. Follow the path across the field, cross over the railway by the footbridge, and then go straight ahead across another field to a fenced track.

17

The heyday of the canals did not last long before the railways supplanted them. The railway cutting dug out to the north of Tring station was also considered one of the great engineering works of the age: one and a half million tons of earth were shifted by men and horses.

3. Turn right and follow the track round past a farm to a T-junction with another track.

4. Turn left into the farmyard and immediately right to a stile by a metal gate. The path then goes half-left, diagonally across the field to a stile by a metal gate in the top left-hand corner.

5. Over the stile, walk towards the near left-hand edge of a hedge seen ahead, and then continue in the same direction, with the hedge on the right. In the corner of the field, go through a hedge gap and a narrow strip of scrub to a stile.

6. The path is not visible on the ground but goes half-left uphill to the top left-hand corner of the field and a stile. It then follows the edge of the wood round to the right, crossing a signed bridleway. Over a stile by a metal gate the path is more obvious and continues just inside the wood.

7. On leaving the wood, bear half-left across fields, crossing two stiles. Over the second stile turn left to yet a third stile onto a lane.

Ahead and right, on top of the hill, can be seen the Bridgewater Monument. This is visited on walk 1, page 12.

 8. Turn right for 200 yards to a signed public bridleway on the left,

Aldbury is a very attractive village

along a track. After 125 yards, cross a stile on the right and walk along the left-hand side of a field towards Aldbury, seen ahead. At the far end of the field continue ahead to a road and carry on in the same direction along the road into the centre of the village. The teashop is at the far end of the pond, opposite the Greyhound.

Aldbury hugs the base of the Chiltern escarpment. It must be one of the most visited and photographed Chiltern villages. It has all the necessary ingredients: a wealth of old and charming buildings in a great variety of styles; a large pond, well supplied with ducks; and a village green, complete with stocks and whipping post. These reminders of a more brutal past were once found on every village green and were used to punish crimes such as playing games on Sunday as well as more serious offences.

9. Continue on the lane through the village.

10. As you approach the end of the village, just before the village car park, turn left on a path signed 'Tring Station 1, Pitstone Hill 1½'. With a tennis court on the right, walk to a stile into a field and continue in the same direction, along the right-hand side of the field, to a small gate in the far right-hand corner and to a T-junction with a track.

11. Turn left and continue along the track, ignoring all side turns, until it joins the Ridgeway (see walk 3, page 24). Carry on in the same direction and after about 70 yards join a surfaced drive to a road.

12. Turn right, back to the start.

Walk 3
THE RIDGEWAY AND TRING

*T*his varied walk starts by exploring a section of the Ridgeway. This long-distance path is a re-creation of the oldest path in Europe and traverses the Chilterns. The route then leaves the Ridgeway and passes through beech woods to a viewpoint with extensive vistas across Aylesbury Vale and the eastern hills of the Chilterns. The route drops down into the attractive old town of Tring, and tea at a fascinating museum. It returns via Tring Park, now in the care of the Woodland Trust.

 The Zebra Café at the Tring branch of the Natural History Museum is appropriately decorated with all sorts of pictures of the animals, and also a photo of Walter Rothschild, the founder of the museum, in a carriage drawn by a zebra. It serves an excellent cream tea with real West Country clotted cream. There is also a selection of cakes, supplemented by a choice of sandwiches, soup, and seasonal specials for lunch. The café is open every day throughout the year, except Christmas Eve, Christmas Day and Boxing Day, between 10.30 am and 5 pm, opening at 2 pm on Sunday. Telephone 020 7942 6178.

DISTANCE: 4 miles.

MAP: OS Explorer 181 Chiltern Hills North, Aylesbury.

STARTING POINT: At the end of Wick Road, Wigginton (GR 936099).

HOW TO GET THERE: From the A41, Tring bypass, follow the signs to Wigginton. At the war memorial, turn right along Chesham Road, and then right again along Wick Road, opposite the Baptist chapel, just before the Greyhound on the right. Go to the very end, where there are several road-side parking spots.

ALTERNATIVE STARTING POINT: If you wish to visit the teashop at the beginning or end of your walk, start in Tring, where there is a car park for the Natural History Museum and other car parks in the town. The teashop is in the museum car park. You will then start the walk at point 7.

THE WALK

It is difficult to believe that this peaceful village was once known as 'Wicked Wigginton'. It was renowned for its liberal publicans, who were said never to turn a customer away, regardless of licensing hours, and cockfights were popular here long after they were banned.

1. Walk along the track, which is the continuation of Wick Road. After a few yards, the Ridgeway path joins on the right. Continue, past Wick Farm, for about ½ mile to a road. Cross the road and continue in the same direction along Church Lane, signed 'Hastoe'.

The Ridgeway is one of the great trade routes of England. It has probably been in use for 4,000 years and is one of the oldest roads in the world. It runs from the Dorset coast to the North Sea and rides the back of one of the six great chalk ridges that radiate from Salisbury Plain. It is thought that this ancient route followed the high chalk land to avoid thick forest and marsh, and along its length prehistoric remains are found in abundance. The Ridgeway path is a modern creation. It was proposed by the Ramblers Association in 1942 and brought into being by the Countryside Commission as one of the long distance routes. The long distance path runs from Ivinghoe Beacon in Buckinghamshire to Overton Hill in Wiltshire. In part it runs along the ancient Ridgeway but also uses other paths. In the Chilterns, it runs mainly along the top of the scarp slope and gives wonderful views out across the Vale of Aylesbury.

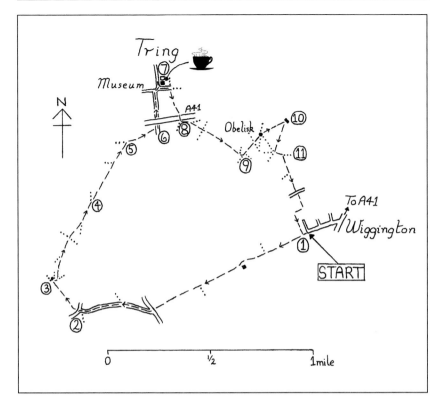

2. At a T-junction turn left along Gadmore Lane and then immediately right on a signed public bridleway.

3. As the track approaches a house (Hastoe Grove), bear right through a wooden gate. Immediately after the gate, turn right, signed 'Hastoe Hill'. After 25 yards, fork left on a faint path, waymarked by a yellow arrow on a post. Follow the waymarks through the bluebell-carpeted wood. Continue ahead when the path merges with one coming in from the left to a fork.

4. The left branch goes downhill inside the wood. Take the right fork, out of the wood, and follow the path along the left-hand side of a field. Press on across the next field. At the far side, there are gaps into two fields. Go through the one on the left and down the right-hand side of a field to meet a cross path.

23

There are extensive views from this part of the walk. To the right can be seen Ivinghoe Beacon and the Bridgewater Monument (see walk 1, page 14), while at your feet is the ancient town of Tring, with the Vale of Aylesbury beyond. Tring lies on Akeman Street, the Roman road from St Albans to Aylesbury and the West. It was granted market rights by Edward II and another charter by Charles II. This prescribed that straw plait be sold in the mornings and corn in the afternoons. Straw plaiting for hats was an important industry in many parts of the Chilterns. The straw needed to be narrow and soft, and the thin Chilterns soils produced suitable raw material in abundance. As a cottage industry it employed large numbers of women and children, and they could earn good money. How much they earned depended on how fast they worked, but their wages compared well with those of agricultural labourers. This gave the women an unusual degree of independence, which was not well received by everyone. The women were accused of being slovenly housewives and, more damming yet, to have a partiality to pretty clothes and loose morals. There is little evidence to substantiate this, but it is true that female literacy lagged behind the rest of the country. This is because girls went to school to learn their craft rather than the three Rs. After 1870, the industry went into rapid decline, due to competition from cheap Chinese straw plait. The workers went into much more poorly paid work on the land or joined the drift to the cities.

5. Turn right and follow the path to a short stretch of surfaced track and a road.

6. Turn left, under Tring bypass, and then, at a T-junction, turn right and follow the road round as it bends left past the zoological museum to the car park and teashop on the right.

In 1872 the Rothschilds bought Tring Mansion. The Rothschilds were well known for their generosity to the town until the estate was sold in 1938. Walter Rothschild was an enthusiastic zoologist and in 1892 he opened the doors of his museum to the public, providing an opportunity to see the greatest and most diverse animal collection ever made by one man. Lord Rothschild was particularly fascinated by big animals and the collection includes examples of the Komodo dragon (the largest living lizard) and the extinct giant moa among its thousands of exhibits ranging from the most commonplace to the rare and unusual. Perhaps the most bizarre is the dressed flea in Gallery 3, in the first closed case. When Walter Rothschild died in 1937 the museum was bequeathed to the Natural History Museum and is now an international centre for ornithological research. It is well worth a visit if you have time and is open from Monday to Saturday, 10 am to 5 pm, and on Sunday from 2 pm to 5 pm (tel: 020 7942 6171).

7. Turn left out of the car park, back past the museum, and then left along Park Road for 100 yards. Turn right on a path signed 'To Tring Park and Wigginton', and use the footbridge to cross the bypass.

8. Turn left for 40 yards and then bear right. The route leads down into a dip and up the other side to a gate into a wood.

This is Tring Park. If you look behind you can see the house, which was built in the reign of Charles II but now has a Victorian facade. The Rothschilds bought it in 1872, and Walter Rothschild stocked the estate with various exotic animals, such as kangaroos and cassowaries. In those days the dangers of introducing exotic species were not so well appreciated as they are now. The edible dormouse, Glis glis, *escaped and is spreading through the Chilterns. It is something of a threat to the native dormouse, because it is bigger and competes successfully for food. When the estate was sold, Hertfordshire County Council bought large areas of woodland to preserve them for public enjoyment, and they are now managed by the Woodland Trust.*

9. Through the gate, turn left on a broad path up to an obelisk. Continue past the obelisk to a classically styled folly.

The obelisk bears no inscription but is locally known as Nell Gwynn's Monument because she is supposed to have stayed in the mansion and walked this way.

10. Turn right up to a gate and path junction. Turn left to a second gate.

11. Go through the gate and then turn immediately right over a stile. You are now back on the Ridgeway. Stay on the Ridgeway path, crossing a drive, to the track along which the walk started. Turn left for a few yards, back to the starting point.

Walk 4
GREAT MISSENDEN AND WENDOVER

*T*his is an exhilarating linear walk between Great Missenden and Wendover, two typical Chiltern towns. It is essentially a ridge walk, and the route is mainly level after the initial, fairly easy climb. There are excellent views all the way and the climax is Coombe Hill, one of the best viewpoints in the Chilterns, which has superb vistas over Aylesbury Vale. Since one of the main features of this outstanding walk is the views, it is essential to choose a clear day to enjoy it at its best. The return is a short train journey over an attractive part of the Chilterns line. (Timetable enquiries: 08705 165165)

 Le Petit Café in Wendover may have a French name and some French influence over the decoration but it is an excellent, essentially English teashop. There are some tables outside in good weather. A variety of set teas, including cream teas, teacake teas and a high tea, are served. There is a tempting selection of cakes and gateaux, as well as scones and teacakes. Choices for lunch include sandwiches, as well as soup, and light meals such as quiches and salad. The café is open every day except Monday, from 9.30 am until 4.30 pm during the week, and until 5.30 pm at the weekend. Telephone 01296 624601.

When the teashop is closed there are several pubs in Wendover that serve food.

DISTANCE: 6½ miles.

MAP: OS Explorer 181 Chiltern Hills North, Aylesbury.

STARTING POINT: Great Missenden station (GR 893013).

HOW TO GET THERE: Great Missenden is just off the A413 Amersham–Aylesbury road. From the A413, take the A4128 High Wycombe road into Great Missenden and follow the signs to the station, where there is a large car park (charge).

ALTERNATIVE STARTING POINT: If you wish to visit the teashop at the beginning or end of your walk, start at Wendover station, where there is ample parking (charge). Turn left out of Station Approach to the teashop. You will then start the walk at point 14.

THE WALK

1. From the station entrance, turn left to the road and then right past some shops to a mini roundabout. Turn left and then right into Walnut Close. Continue in the same direction on a path at the end. This goes past a car park on the right to a stile.

Great Missenden once had a great abbey, the largest in Buckinghamshire. Our route does not pass the abbey, but it can clearly be seen on looking back towards the town. It was founded by William de Missenden in 1133 and was the source of several scandals. Hugh de Plessetis, lord of the manor in the 13th century, was buried in the churchyard, together with his white palfrey, Principal, his armour, and the horse's harness. In 1297 a novice cut his own throat 'for fear of discipline', and one of the abbots was hanged for clipping the coins of Edward III! In 1530 there was another scandal when Abbot John Fox faced heavy charges against his community, one of whom 'had been seen more than once coming out of a house in the village in doublet and jerkin with a sword by his side'.

The abbey fell prey to the Dissolution in 1534 and the last abbot, John Otwell, accepted the inevitable and returned to secular life with a pension of £50 a year. James Oldham, a London ironmonger, bought the decayed estate in 1787 and constructed the building we see today, which incorporates a few traces of the original monastery. It is now used as a residential study centre.

2. Over the stile turn left. Cross two further stiles, and continue in the same direction across a large field, ignoring a path over a stile to the right, to find a stile about 50 yards from the far right corner. The field you now enter is used as a caravan park and for balloon rallies. Bear left to the road at the Black Horse.

You are now walking up the valley of the River Missbourne, which apparently rises in a pond we shall pass and flows 14 miles southeast to the Coln, near Uxbridge. History records that it has changed its course more than once, each change being said to presage a national disaster! The river is a poor thing today, dry in some parts, and in others no more than a trickle. Its name – a combination of British maes *'field' and Old English* burna *'spring', 'stream' – is particularly appropriate for a river whose course is often marked just by a grass grown dip in the field, as you can see to your left. In 1774 it was recorded as being 30 feet wide! It had a reputation for quirkiness even then. Old accounts tell of it running dry in wet winters and being in spate in times of drought. A book issued by the Chiltern Society in 1987 called* To Rescue a River *blames the present sad state of the river on over-abstraction. Such a fuss has been made about this that efforts are being made to correct it but much of the river is still dry.*

3. Turn right for 40 yards and then turn left on a signed footpath. Go straight ahead under the railway to a stile.

A pond on the left, which may be dried up, is said to be the source of the Missbourne. It has had much work done on it by the Chiltern Society.

Over the stile, bear right to the right-hand one of two visible stiles. Cross the next field on a very well defined path to some steps at the far end. At the top of the steps, continue up in the same direction, and at the end of the field follow the path through a wood.

4. At a T-junction at the end of the wood, turn right. Follow the hedged path and then press on along the left-hand side of a field. Ahead right is an excellent view of Wendover Woods, which is the highest point of the Chilterns. At the far side of the field continue on into a wood, ignoring a path on the right.

5. At the end of the wood continue on a path between hedges. This

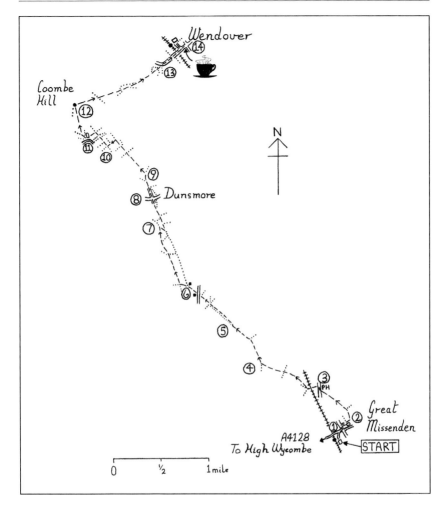

may sometimes be very muddy. If so, it can be avoided by taking a parallel path over a stile in the fields on the left. Cross a track, and then a road at Cobblers Hill Farm, and continue in the same direction. After 150 yards the track ends at a house called Colenso.

6. Cross a stile on the left and cut across the corner of the small field to another stile. Over this, continue in the same direction across a field to a stile part way along the fence opposite. Cross the stile, and after 75 yards turn right along a crossing path. Follow this as it contours along the hillside, with magnificent views on the left, for a good half mile to a stile.

7. Do not cross the stile, but turn sharp right, almost back on yourself, and go gently uphill to a track. Turn left.

8. Cross a lane and continue along the lane opposite into Dunsmore. Carry on as the road becomes a track. Ignore the first public footpath on the left, but continue to a second after another 100 yards.

9. Bear left. This path goes between wire fences, and eventually the fence on the right becomes a tall deer fence. Watch for a gap in this fence, protected by a cattle grid, at a junction with a broad bridleway on the left. Carry on by the deer fence for a further 170 yards, and then turn left for 200 yards. The junction is marked by yellow arrows on a tree.

10. Turn right. Ignore several unmarked side turns and cross paths and continue for 300 yards until you come to a cross path marked by a yellow arrow on a tree, somewhat to the left. Turn left and follow the path to a car park.

11. Cross the car park to a wooden gate; take the centre one of three paths for 100 yards; and then bear right to the monument on Coombe Hill.

Coombe Hill is the highest viewpoint of the Chilterns but it is not the highest point. That lies three miles away in Wendover Woods. There are excellent views over the Vale of Aylesbury. It is said that you could see St Paul's Cathedral before the hill was covered with trees, but I doubt it. The monument is to 148 soldiers who died in the Boer War. The original metal plaque was stolen; so now the names are engraved in the stone. The chalk grassland, heath, and wood are included in a Site of Special Scientific Interest.

12. Turn right and go slightly downhill to a post with the Ridgeway symbol – a white acorn. (See walk 3, page 22.) Follow the main path down to a road. For some reason, at one point the Ridgeway path is signed to the left off the main path, but it rejoins the main path a little further on.

13. Turn right along the road into Wendover, passing the station on the left, to the teashop on the right.

Wendover is a very ancient town, first mentioned in a will in 970, when the Anglo Saxon name Wændofran *was used. However, it is certainly older than that, as it lies in an important gap in the hills. On the High Street is the Manor Waste, Wendover's equivalent of a village green. Much damage was being done to it by indiscriminate car parking, and so the council paved it with slabs and cobbles, planted trees and provided seats. Wendover has two fairs a year on the site: one in spring and one in autumn. Their charter dates back to 1214. The market on the Waste, on Thursday, is based on a 14th century charter and has recently been reinstated. It is worth wandering round Wendover, as there are many old buildings that appear to have hardly altered over the years. Many of these can be found in the streets surrounding the High Street. One is the Red Lion, an ancient coaching inn and a meeting point for the local councillors. Records date it to 1670, although it is likely to be very much older.*

The borough returned two burgesses to Parliament in the early 14th century but allowed this privilege to lapse until 1625. It was then the smallest borough in England but had a remarkably distinguished list of representatives, including, at different times, Edmund Burke, George Canning, and John Hampden. In nearby Great Kimble church is a framed copy of the report of parish overseers setting out the names of those who refused to pay a tax known as ship money. It is headed by John Hampden, and his subsequent arrest and trial was one of the causes of the Civil War.

14. Turn left out of the teashop and retrace your steps to Wendover Station, turning right along Station Approach, to catch the train to Great Missenden.

Walk 5
THE KINGSHILLS

This pleasant walk explores the countryside round Great and Little Kingshill. It is mainly fairly level and easy going, with long stretches in pleasant woodland. The high spot of the walk comes early in the second half with an outstanding view over the Hughenden Valley.

The area explored on this walk was once famous for its cherry orchards – alas, no more. The Limes at Hildreth Garden Centre acknowledges this with cherry ladders suspended from the ceiling of its pleasant, modern interior. There are also some tables outside overlooking the plant displays. On offer is a tempting and enterprising menu with a good selection of cakes and individual fruit tarts. For lunch there is a choice of sandwiches, pannini, and omelettes, as well as daily specials displayed on a blackboard. Opening hours are between 9 am and 5 pm during the week, and from 9.30 am to 4.30 pm on Sunday. Telephone 01494 865300.

DISTANCE: 5½ miles.

MAP: OS Explorer 172 Chiltern Hills East, High Wycombe, Maidenhead.

STARTING POINT: Great Kingshill car park (GR 877982).

HOW TO GET THERE: From the A4128, High Wycombe–Prestwood road, turn east at Great Kingshill along a minor road to a signed car park.

ALTERNATIVE STARTING POINT: If you wish to visit the teashop at the beginning or end of your walk, start at Hildreth Garden Centre, also on the A4128, where there is a large car park. The teashop is in the garden centre. Permission should be sought before leaving a car for an extended period. You will then start the walk at point 12.

THE WALK

1. Return to the entrance to the car park, cross the road and bear left across the common to an exit in the far left corner, beyond the swings.

The area round Great Kingshill once used to be famous for its cherry orchards but they have disappeared under modern development, together with the customs that went with them like the cherry pie feasts.

2. Turn right along the lane for 20 yards and then turn left on a signed path. Follow this path across a field, between houses, across a road, and then ahead between fences to a stile. Over the stile, press on along the right-hand side of a field to another stile. Over this stile, go ahead for a few yards; then bear left to walk along the left-hand side of a field, and continue across a second field and through a gap in a hedge to a cross path.

3. Turn right.

4. Watch for a stile on the right; immediately before it, turn left on a fenced path that leads through to a road. Cross the road and go ahead on a signed path along a farm track.

5. At Cope's Farm, bear right over a stile beside a field gate and follow the path along the left-hand side of three fields to a stile into a wood. Continue along the left-hand side of the wood and then ahead on a fenced path to a lane.

6. Turn left.

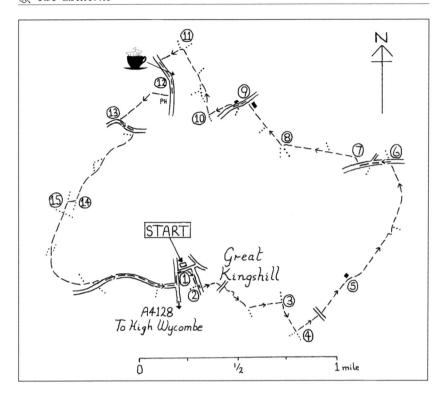

7. Some 120 yards after Hare Lane, turn right along a track. When the track ends, continue over a stile by a field gate to a second stile and ahead for 50 yards. Now fork left across a field to a stile onto a cross path.

8. Turn right and carry on past a farm shop to a road.

9. Turn left. About 50 yards after Peterley Lodge, take a signed path on the right into woodland. When this forks, take either branch, as they both shortly lead to a clear cross path.

10. Turn right. Follow the main path to a T-junction, ignoring all side paths.

☕ **11.** Turn left, waymarked by a yellow arrow on a post, and then left again after 10 yards, to walk with a wooden fence on the left. This leads to a road. Turn left to the garden centre and teashop on the left.

12. Turn left out of the teashop to continue along the road. Immediately before the Polecat Inn, turn right on a signed path that starts through the pub car park. Over a stile, follow the path across a field and downhill to a stile onto a lane.

There are wonderful views of Hughenden Valley from this part of the walk and one can understand why Disraeli chose it as his home (see walk 6, page 40).

13. Turn left. Opposite the entrance to Warren Field, turn right on a signed path into Longfield Wood. Follow the path ahead, ignoring a path on the right after 5 yards. When the path forks, take the upper branch for about 400 yards.

14. The next junction is easy to miss but important. Watch for a white arrow on a tree that indicates a path bearing right, downhill. (It is not very obvious, especially in autumn when the paths are obscured by leaves.) Follow this path, using the white arrows to guide you, down to a cross path contouring round the hillside at a lower level.

15. Turn left. Continue over two stiles and a cross path. When the path forks, follow the waymarked path left, uphill. Press on ahead when the path joins a track that leads to a lane, and carry on in the same direction along the lane to the main road. Turn left and then right, back to the car park where this walk started.

Walk 6
HUGHENDEN VALLEY

Benjamin Disraeli knew and loved the Chilterns, making his home at Hughenden, just outside High Wycombe. This walk explores the beautiful valley he chose and visits his home for tea.

 The Stable Restaurant at Hughenden Manor provides the usual excellent National Trust fare. The menu is based around dishes historically relevant to Hughenden and is inspired by Victorian recipes. Local produce is used as much as possible, including fruit, vegetables, and herbs from the estate. Perhaps most notable among the cakes is Hughenden applecake, made, when available, with apples from the estate orchard, which is planted with old varieties. There is a tempting selection of other cakes, scones, and crumpets, as well as cream teas. Lunches are served between noon and 2 pm and include a stable lad's lunch with local cheeses or fidget pie. This is a traditional pie of bacon, potato, and apple, baked with rosemary in a cold-water crust. A variety of teas is available, and hot chocolate with cream is tempting on a cold day. On a hot day you might prefer one of the traditional cold drinks, such as lemonade or ginger beer. Stable Restaurant is open from noon until 5 pm on Wednesday to Sunday in the summer and at the weekend in winter, opening and closing an hour earlier in the darkest days of winter. Telephone: 01494 755576. (There is no other source of refreshment on this route.)

DISTANCE: 4 miles.

MAP: OS Explorer 172 Chiltern Hills East, High Wycombe, Maidenhead.

STARTING POINT: Car park opposite 272/274 Hughenden Road, High Wycombe (GR 865944).

HOW TO GET THERE: Hughenden Road is the A4128, High Wycombe–Prestwood road. The car park is on the edge of High Wycombe and is not signed.

ALTERNATIVE STARTING POINT: If you wish to visit the teashop at the beginning or end of your walk, start in the car park at Hughenden Manor. The teashop is in the stable block, between the car park and the manor and gardens. You will then start the walk at point 8.

THE WALK

1. Facing the road, leave the car park by a surfaced path on the left and follow the path to a small bridge across a stream.

2. Across the bridge, turn right to walk with the stream on your right. There is no path on the ground; this area is open access, and you are free to wander at will. A gate takes you onto the National Trust land. After passing through a second gate, bear slightly left away from the stream to pass to the right of a church.

There has been a church here since the 12th century but not much remains of the old structure, as it was extensively restored in Disraeli's time. It has a fine series of tombs, which are curiosities because they are forgeries, carried out by a local family, the Wellesbournes, in Tudor times, to try to establish a connection with the great family of de Montfort. Disraeli is buried in the churchyard, in the family vault. We are also told that a Mrs Sarah Brydges-Willyams is buried there. Disraeli was perpetually short of money. When Mrs Brydges-Willyams, a staunch, if eccentric, admirer, offered him £30,000 if she could be buried beside him, Disraeli accepted the money. In the church is a memorial plaque placed there by his most famous admirer, 'his grateful and affectionate sovereign and friend, Victoria R.I.'. Queen Victoria visited Hughenden several times, including the occasion of a royal visit to High Wycombe in 1877 when the local bodgers, or chair-makers, built a huge arch of chairs across the road. There is a drawing of the event in the study in the house.

3. Cross the drive to the church and a drive to Hughenden Manor. Keep ahead, signed 'Hughenden Valley', to a metal kissing gate by a field gate; then press ahead in the same direction along the right-hand side of three fields. Continue across a fourth field until you are level with a metal kissing gate on the left and a roundabout on the road to the right.

4. Turn left up to the gate. Through the gate, go ahead a few yards to a cross path. Do not take the obvious path bearing left. Instead, turn right for 3 yards and then left again through a wooden kissing gate. Follow the path uphill along the right-hand side of a field to a kissing gate on the right. Go through the gate and carry on uphill, now with a hedge on the left and allotments on the right.

5. Turn right in front of a fence on a signed path. In a dip in front of a house, follow the path to the left, over a stile. At the end of the garden on the right, continue uphill to a stile in the top right-hand corner of the field. Go ahead on a fenced path to a road.

6. Cross the road and turn left along the footway.

☕ **7.** At a road junction, turn left on a signed path along Church Lane. This shortly becomes an unsurfaced track. Follow this into woodland, past the National Trust car park for Hughenden Manor, and then ahead on a surfaced drive. Bear left down a path and some steps to the signed teashop.

Hughenden Manor was the home of Benjamin Disraeli, the favourite prime minister of Queen Victoria. He bought it for £35,000 and lived there for 33 years. The house and 190 acres of parkland were acquired by the National Trust in 1946. The house is packed with his belongings, including manuscripts of his novels and labels sent with primroses by Queen Victoria. The study is much as he left it at his death in 1881. His early struggles to enter Parliament are in complete contrast to his later success. He spent much of his youth at Bradenham Manor, just over the hill (see walk 8, page 52) and, in 1832, he

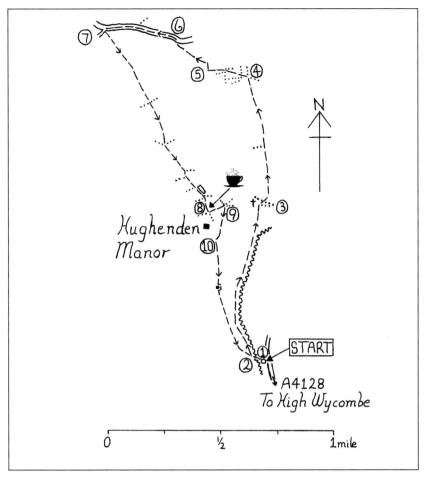

stood as an Independent candidate in a by-election in nearby Wycombe. He was defeated despite a flamboyant campaign featuring his colours of pink and white. He tried again at the general election in December of the same year and was so convinced of his success that he had a pink and white chair made to carry him round the town in triumph. But again he lost! He tried a third time, with the same result and came to the conclusion that he could only succeed if he joined one of the political parties. He objected to the Tories least and so picked them. In 1837 he was elected as MP for Maidstone, following the death of the sitting member, his friend Wyndham Lewis. The citizens of Wycombe overcame their objections and subscribed to illuminations in his honour! He was prime minister from 1878 to 1880 and was given the title Earl of Beaconsfield.

Disraeli knew he needed money to further his political ambitions. Not only had his friend bequeathed him a winnable seat, he also left a rich widow, Mary Ann, and Disraeli started to court her. At first she irritated him with her chatter but they came to love each other deeply. In later years Mary Ann said to a friend, 'Dizzy married me for my money, but if he had the chance again, he would marry me for love.' He was inconsolable, when she died, and the Hughenden notepaper afterwards had a black border.

The park in which the manor stands is shared with Wycombe District Council. The house is open to the public on Wednesday to Saturday and Bank Holiday Mondays, from 2 pm till 6 pm, between April and October, and at weekends in March (telephone 01494 532580).

8. Leave the stable yard through double gates. At a T-junction with a drive, turn left, downhill.

9. At a junction with a drive on the left, which is the entrance to the car park, bear right off the drive and through a small wooden gate. Through the gate, turn right along the top of the slope, passing the manor house on the right. Through a metal kissing gate, go ahead to meet a grassy track, once one of the entrances to Hughenden Manor.

10. Turn left. When the track ends at a lodge, bear left round the garden and then right, to resume walking along the track. Bear left to the bridge crossed at the start of the walk and retrace your steps to the car park. (If you started at Hughenden Manor, do not cross the bridge but turn left to walk by the stream.)

Walk 7
STUDLEY GREEN

This walk embodies so much that is delightful about walking in the Chilterns, exploring dry valleys surrounded by hills crowned with woods known as hangers. The route is simply summarised: up one valley; over the top, stopping for tea; and back down another valley. The return leg is exceptional, as it includes the outstanding Bottom Wood, managed by the Chiltern Society, and beautiful at any time of year.

Blooms Garden Centre at Studley Green has an excellent and deservedly popular teashop. It is unpretentious and pleasant, with charming touches, such as fresh flowers on the tables even in the depths of winter. There are some tables outside in an enclosed and sheltered garden. It serves a good selection of tempting cakes and these are supplemented by a choice of sandwiches, baguettes, and filled jacket potatoes. If the Chiltern air has given you more of an appetite, there is also a daily special, such as a satisfying shepherd's pie. The teashop is open from 9.30 am until 4.30 pm every day except Christmas Day, Boxing Day, and Good Friday, closing a little earlier in winter. Tel: 01494 485965.

DISTANCE: 4½ miles.

MAP: OS Explorer 171 Chiltern Hills West, Henley-on-Thames & Wallingford.

HOW TO GET THERE: The starting point is on the A40 High Wycombe – Oxford road 1½ miles west of West Wycombe. There is plenty of space to park on a service road near the Dashwood Arms.

STARTING POINT: The Dashwood Arms near Piddington (GR 807943).

ALTERNATIVE STARTING POINT: If you wish to visit the teashop at the beginning or end of your walk, there is a car park at Blooms Garden Centre, which is on the A40 east of Stokenchurch. Permission should be sought before leaving a car for a lengthy period. You will then start the walk at point 9.

THE WALK

1. Turn left up Chipps Hill for 50 yards; then turn right on a signed public bridleway. At a farm continue ahead, now along the right-hand side of a field. At the end of the field, follow the main track round to the right for 200 yards, to a stile into a wood on the right. Do not cross the stile but continue along the track as it now bears left and eventually leads to a gate into a wood.

2. Follow the path through the wood; it is clearly defined and marked by occasional white arrows on trees. About 600 yards after entering the wood, watch for a cross path marked by white arrows on a beech tree. Take the path right, marked S51. This is about 30 yards before a minor lane.

3. At the top of the hill, branch half-left, following the path marked by white arrows.

4. The path takes a sharp turn right and leads into a complex of buildings. Follow the signed path ahead to a drive.

This complex of buildings is the U.K. headquarters of the Wycliffe Bible Translators. William Cameron Townsend, a missionary to the Cakchiquel Indians of Guatemala, founded the movement in 1942. He had the idea when a Cakchiquel man challenged him: 'If your God is so great, why doesn't he

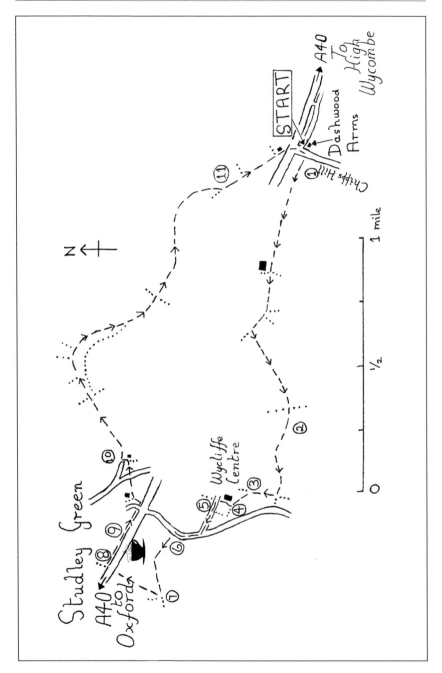

START

A40
To
High
Wycombe

Dashwood
Arms

Chitphs Hill

N

1 mile

½

0

Wycliffe
Centre

Studley Green

A40
to
Oxford

speak in my language?' The name comes from the pre-Reformation hero, John Wycliffe, who first translated the Bible into English.

5. Turn left along the drive and then right along a minor road for 200 yards.

6. Turn left on a signed public footpath along Copse Drive. At the entrance to The Coppins the path goes between a fence and a wall. Cross a stile and go half-left across a field to a stile into a wood at the far side.

7. Go ahead for 30 yards; then turn right on a path, marked with the usual white arrows, that runs more or less parallel with the edge of the wood.

8. At the A40 turn right to Blooms Garden Centre and the teashop.

9. Turn right along the A40 for 200 yards. Some 20 yards after St Francis Road, turn left on a signed public footpath down the drive to a house called Nutfield. In front of Nutfield fork right. Continue on this path across a minor road. At a track in front of The Cottage turn left.

10. At a T-junction after 70 yards, turn right on a public bridleway signed 'Bottom Wood 1 km'. Press on as it enters Bottom Wood and follow this path along the valley for about a mile, ignoring all side paths. The path can be muddy and there is a parallel walkers' route to the right, that allows you to escape the worst of it and eventually rejoin the main track. Leave the wood and continue in the same direction across a field.

Bottom Wood belongs to the Chiltern Society and is used as a demonstration wood. It covers 14.5 hectares, of which 11.5 hectares are ancient woodland. When it was taken over in 1983 it was neglected and in a poor state but it has been transformed into a thriving wood with a patchwork of trees of different ages and a profusion of woodland flowers. A total of 703 species of animal and plant have been recorded, including 19 mammals, 52 birds, 26 butterflies, 300 moths, and 190 flowering plants.

It has a thriving population of dormice, which are now rare over most of

Britain. The dormice in Bottom Wood are the native common species, not the much larger, edible dormouse, an introduced species that also lives in the Chilterns (see walk 3, page 25). The common dormouse is about three inches long plus another 2½ inches of tail. It has orange fur and its tail is thick and hairy. It weighs just half an ounce, but may be twice as heavy when it has stoked up for hibernation. Dormice eat pollen and nectar from flowers; insects; and various fruits and nuts. Mostly these are high-energy foods, and differ from the seeds that most mice eat. Many things that dormice feed on are only available for a short period each year. This means they need a varied habitat so that a succession of foods can be used through their active season. This suits many other kinds of wildlife; so dormice act as a barometer for the health of our woodlands. During the 20th century, the dormouse disappeared from many parts of the country where it used to live, as disappearing woodlands and hedgerows and changes in woodland management made life difficult for this tiny mammal.

11. After passing through a gate at the far end of the field, carry on along the track, past a farm, and back to the A40 at the Dashwood Arms.

Walk 8
BRADENHAM AND WEST WYCOMBE

*Th*is *walk connects two villages, both attractive, though very different, and both in the care of the National Trust. Starting in Bradenham, the outward route makes its way through some beautiful woodland to West Wycombe. After the tea halt, the route climbs the hill overlooking West Wycombe, and there is an exhilarating ridge walk before a steep descent to Bradenham. Allow plenty of time for this expedition because there are so many interesting things to see at West Wycombe and such wonderful views to enjoy.*

 The teashop featured on this walk is in West Wycombe Garden Centre, which itself has been developed with an ancient walled garden that has been in existence since before 1775. It has been producing plants and food crops for all that time, making it probably the oldest garden of its kind in the country. The light, modern interior of the teashop is decorated with interesting notices about the custom of afternoon tea. The best feature is the patio, and the views from here are the best of any teashop in the Chilterns. There are old-fashioned sweets in jars to be bought, as well as an excellent selection of delicious cakes to choose from – or maybe a cream tea will tempt you – and there is a choice of sandwiches or filled jacket potatoes for a light lunch. The teashop is open every day from 8.30 am during the week and 11 am on Sundays, closing in the summer at 5.30 pm during the week and 5 pm on Sunday, and perhaps a little earlier in winter. Telephone: 01494 438638.

DISTANCE: 5 miles.

MAP: OS Explorer 172 Chiltern Hills East, High Wycombe, Maidenhead.

STARTING POINT: National Trust car park at Bradenham (GR 827969).

HOW TO GET THERE: From the A4010 High Wycombe–Aylesbury road, 1½ miles north of its junction with the A40, take a minor road signed 'Bradenham'. Take the first lane on the right for 50 yards; then turn left on a track beside the village green to a car park.

ALTERNATIVE STARTING POINT: If you wish to visit the teashop at the beginning or end of your walk, start in West Wycombe, where there is ample parking in a public car park on Chorley Road. The teashop is in the garden centre adjacent to the car park. You will then start the walk at point 9.

THE WALK

1. Return to the track and turn left. When the track forks after 200 yards, take the right branch (not the footpath on the right at this point) and follow the track up through woods.

2. When the track bends sharp right, continue ahead on a path for about 150 yards to a fork by a notice board. Bear right for 100 yards to a cross path.

3. Turn right and follow this path to a stile on the right, ignoring a path on the right after 140 yards.

4. Turn right over the stile and follow the path down a small valley to a gate. The path does not go through the gate. Instead, turn left to walk, with a fence on the right, down to a track in a dip and up the other side, still with a fence on the right; over another cross track; and on to a farm. Go ahead on a track to pass to the right of farm buildings to a surfaced drive.

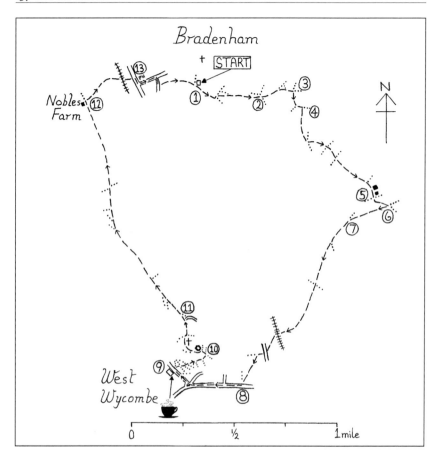

5. Cross the drive to a small gate and follow the path through woodland to a broad, grassy cross path.

6. Turn right down a valley to a surfaced drive.

7. Turn left along the drive for 200 yards. When the drive bends left, continue ahead along a signed path that shortly heads across a large field. At the far side, cross a track and press on along the path, eventually going under a railway and across a field to a main road. Cross the road and take a signed path on the other side. This goes along the right-hand side of a field for 50 yards and then bears left across the field to a gate onto a road.

8. Turn right through West Wycombe. At the far end of the village, opposite the entrance to West Wycombe park, turn right along Chorley Road, signed 'Bledlow Ridge 3', to the garden centre and teashop on the left.

West Wycombe, in the care of the National Trust since the 1930s, is exceptionally picturesque, with examples of many types of English architecture from the 16th century onwards. It is well worth taking the time to explore in detail with the aid of the architectural trail guide published by the National Trust and available from the village shop. The George and Dragon is an old coaching inn. At the rear are ancient pigeon lofts which used to house birds kept by the owner to carry messages to and from London and Oxford when wet weather made the coach journey slow or even impossible. It is reputed to be haunted by the ghost of a barmaid who fell in love with a rich gentleman. She received a note, apparently from her lover, asking her to meet him so they could elope. In fact the note was a cruel trick by local lads. She turned up only to meet the lads teasing her, laughing and throwing stones. One missile struck her on the head and killed her. Her ghost has been seen in the pub even in modern times.

The late Sir Francis Dashwood gave West Wycombe House and park to the National Trust in 1943. A previous Sir Francis, the second baronet, formed the Dilletante Society, a group dedicated to the study of classical architecture. Between 1740 and 1781, he transformed the earlier house to reflect his interests and it is an outstanding example of neo-classical architecture. The interior continues the classical theme and is richly decorated. The hall and staircase are considered to be like a roman atrium. The saloon has a painted ceiling depicting the Council of the Gods. In the blue drawing room, the painted ceiling shows the triumph of Bacchus and Ariadne. There are fine marble fireplaces and a staircase of mahogany, walnut and satinwood. The house contains fine tapestries, family portraits, and some splendid 18th century furniture. It is open to the public in June, July, and August, Sunday to Thursday, from 2 pm until 6 pm. The grounds only are also open in April and May on Wednesday and Sunday afternoons. Tel: 01494 524411.

This Sir Francis succeeded to his father's estate and fortune when he was only 16. A man of considerable energy, wealth and achievement, not to say profligacy, he was Chancellor of the Exchequer (said at the time to be the worst ever) and Postmaster General. He rewrote the Book of Common Prayer *in everyday English. Today his popular reputation is associated solely with the Hellfire Club, which was supposedly founded for the practice of black magic, first at Medmenham Abbey and then in the caves that are now signed from the*

The mausoleum on West Wycombe Hill

village and open to the public. The name the group gave themselves was the Brotherhood of St Francis or Dashwood's Apostles, and half of Dashwood's cabinet colleagues were members. They were undoubtedly up to no good, but wild parties are more likely than devil worship. The caves are not natural; they were the byproduct of excavations to provide raw materials for the new road to High Wycombe that Dashwood built to relieve local poverty and unemployment. They extend into the hillside for about a quarter of a mile and have been cleaned out, lit and provided with displays designed to recreate times past.

9. Return to the road, cross it, and take the path ahead, ignoring a left branch after 5 yards. After 50 yards, go down two steps, across a path, and up six steps on the other side. Go ahead for a further 10 yards; then bear left uphill.

10. At the top turn left to the mausoleum and pass to the left of the monument. Fork right to the church with its crowning golden ball; then go ahead through the churchyard to a gate onto an open area used as a car park. When the track across this area bears right, go ahead between low wooden posts to meet another track.

West Wycombe hill was once crowned by an Iron Age hill fort, and the fortifications can be seen running parallel with the churchyard fence and at the eastern end are cut by the mausoleum. The mausoleum is really a folly and contains memorials to members of the Dashwood family and their friends.

50

St Lawrence's church was originally the parish church of Haveringdon. This was once a little way along the ridge and was abandoned in the late 18th century, probably as a consequence of a lack of water. Only the ruined chancel and part of the tower remained when Sir Francis Dashwood turned his attention to it. The nave is like a neo-classical drawing room, the ceiling has a huge solar mandala, and everywhere the imagery is of suns and serpents, reflecting the tastes perhaps of the widely travelled Sir Francis Dashwood. The most unusual feature of all is the golden ball on top of the tower. It holds perhaps eight people and members of the Hellfire Club used to play cards there. John Wilkes, a friend of Dashwood's, described it as 'the best Globe tavern I was ever in'. You can visit the church, including the golden ball, on some summer weekends.

11. Turn left along the track. When it forks after a bare ½ mile, bear right and follow the track along the ridge for a further ½ mile to Nobles Farm.

12. Some 15 yards after the track becomes surfaced, turn right off the track and follow a path downhill, across the railway line, to the main road.

13. Turn right for 50 yards; then left at the Red Lion, back to Bradenham. After 200 yards, take the first lane on the right for 50 yards; then turn left on a track beside the village green, back to the car park where this walk started.

Bradenham must come close to everyone's ideal of an English village, with the manor house and church looking out across the village green, complete with cricket pitch and surrounded by pretty cottages. It has been in the care of the National Trust since 1956. Bradenham Manor was rented by Isaac d'Israeli from 1829 until his death in 1848, while his famous son was rising to high office. It was Benjamin who dropped the d-apostrophe. Isaac d'Israeli was a distinguished man in his own right and an authority on antiquarian books. Jewish by ancestry, he became a member of the Anglican church along with his children, and the church next to the Manor House, St Botolph's, has a memorial to him. The church was originally Saxon but of course has alterations and additions from every age. It boasts two of the oldest bells in England, dating from 1250, and has the usual informatory booklet within. Another distinction of Bradenham is that it is one of the very few places to remain in the possession of its Saxon owners after the Norman Conquest, though they did acquire a Norman overlord.

Walk 9
SEER GREEN AND CHALFONT ST GILES

*T*his varied walk uses the footpaths linking two prosperous and attractive Chiltern villages with contrasting histories, one ancient and one modern. Hodgemoor Wood, on the first part of the route, is exceptionally attractive, but never more so than in early May, when it is carpeted with bluebells. There are some fine views of typical Chilterns scenery.

The teashop on this walk, Tea Time, is in the centre of Chalfont St Giles. It is a traditional village teashop, overlooking the village green, and has some tables outside at the front in summer. It sells a good range of cakes, and there is a choice of sandwiches, soup, or filled jacket potatoes for a light lunch. Tea Time is open from 9.30 am to 5.30 pm, Monday to Saturday, and 2.30 pm to 5.30 pm on Sunday throughout the year. Tel: 01494 871099.

DISTANCE: 6 miles.

MAP: OS Explorer 172 Chiltern Hills East, High Wycombe, Maidenhead.

STARTING POINT: Holy Trinity Church in Seer Green (GR 966919).

HOW TO GET THERE: From the A355 Beaconsfield–Amersham road, 1 mile north of its junction with the A40, take a minor road signed 'Seer Green'. After about a mile, turn left on a road, again signed 'Seer Green'. Park in the centre of the village near the church.

ALTERNATIVE STARTING POINT: If you wish to visit the teashop at the beginning or end of your walk, start in Chalfont St Giles, where there is some street parking. You will then start the walk at point 10.

The Walk

Seer Green was mentioned in Domesday Book as La Sere. It was a hamlet until the coming of the railway made it a convenient place for London commuters to live.

1. Take the road past the Three Horseshoes and the shops (Orchard Road). Next to number 27 on the right is a signed footpath. Follow this, between houses and across two roads, to emerge in a field.

2. Bear diagonally left to a stile. Over the stile, turn right on a fenced path to a second stile. Cross the stile and continue ahead on the right-hand side of two fields with a wood on the right. Go over yet another stile and follow the path ahead to a lane.

3. Turn right for about ¼ mile, passing Rawlings Farm.

4. When the lane bends sharply right, there are several signed footpaths and horse trails into Hodgemoor wood on the left. Turn left into the wood, and after 10 yards fork right. After a further 25 yards, branch left on a broad track. Follow this through the wood, ignoring all side branches, for about ½ mile. Eventually the main track bends right with a smaller path ahead. Stay on the main track round to the right, and then to the left and ahead, to a cross path where the right branch is barred by a wooden barrier after 30 yards.

5. Continue ahead, now on a path. After 100 yards follow the main path round to the left; then, after a further 30 yards, bear right to a major track.

6. Turn left. After 50 yards, when the track bears left, continue ahead through a wooden barrier and press on in the same direction to meet a lane on a corner. (Note: it is very easy to miss the path in Hodgemore Wood as it is a maze of unmarked paths. If this happens, head north to come out on a lane, and turn right to pick up the route at point 7.)

7. Turn right to continue in the same direction along the lane. At a right-hand bend, go through a small wooden gate on a signed path and keep going in the same direction. Walk along the left-hand side of the field. The views to the right extend as far as London on a clear day. At the far end of the field, go over a stile and follow a broad path between fences to a T-junction.

8. Turn right for 20 yards; then turn left on a track. (Do not be misled by the signs to Chalfont St Giles; the route described has better views and is a more attractive way into the village.) After Dairy Cottage the track becomes a path between hedges. Cross a stile and continue down the right-hand side of a field. Go over a stile on the right. In this field the path is not visible on the ground. Go ahead and slightly right to a stile in the fence at the far side, and ahead for 25 yards to a T-junction.

9. Turn right and follow the path to a lane. Keep ahead in the same direction along the lane for 60 yards; then go along a track signed 'South Bucks Way' when the lane bends left. When the track ends, continue ahead on a path. It eventually becomes a track again leading into the middle of Chalfont St Giles. The teashop is across the road, slightly left.

Chalfont St Giles was a much more substantial community than Seer Green before the growth of commuting, though, in common with all the villages in this part of the Chilterns, it has seen considerable expansion in modern times. The centre of Chalfont St Giles is still very picturesque, with its village green surrounded by old cottages, shops, and pubs. The church, reached through a gate by the teashop, is of 12th century origin and has some famous medieval wall paintings. The graveyard has an unusually wide variety of headstones and memorials, many bearing epitaphs. One was obviously written for someone who felt he had travelled far enough:

Italy and Spain, Germany and France,
Have been on earth my weary Dance.
So that I own the grave's my dearest Friend
That to my travels it has put an End.

10. From the teashop turn left and walk up the road for about 400 yards, passing Milton's Cottage.

The most famous building in Chalfont St Giles is Milton's Cottage. From the name – and because it is a museum full of Milton memorabilia – you might imagine that the poet spent all his life here. In fact, he lived in the house for nine months in the plague year of 1665. The house was found for him by his pupil and friend Thomas Ellwood, and while living here Milton finished Paradise Lost *and started* Paradise Regained. *The museum has first editions of both books, as well as other exhibits, and a beautifully maintained and charming cottage garden. The cottage is the only house still in existence where Milton is known to have lived. It was bought by public subscription in 1887 to commemorate Queen Victoria's Jubilee with the queen herself heading the subscription list with £20. From March to October, it is open Tuesday to Saturday, from 10 am to 1 pm and from 2 pm to 5 pm, and on Sunday from 2 pm to 5 pm.*

11. Just before Hillside Close, take a signed footpath on the left. Follow this uphill, ignoring a footpath on the left, to emerge on a playing field. Carry on along the left-hand side, and at the far end continue ahead, with the bowling club hut on the right. Beyond the bowling green, carry on along the left-hand side of the field to a gate onto a track.

12. Take a signed footpath immediately opposite and follow it to a road, ignoring a branch on the left after ½ mile.

13. Cross the road and take the path directly opposite over a substantial stile. When the path forks after 100 yards, bear right. After a further 125 yards, follow the path as it bears left. When the wood on the left ends, do not cross the stile but carry on along the fenced path to a stile by a metal field gate. Over the stile, press on along the right-hand side of four small fields and along a broad, tree-lined path to a road.

14. Turn right for 120 yards and then left up a signed path along a track. At the end of the track, cross a stile ahead and bear right along the right-hand side of a field. At the end of the field, go through a wooden kissing gate. After 25 yards turn left on a cross path through another kissing gate. Carry on ahead when this leads onto a playing field.

15. In the corner of the playing field, press on along the path. Ignore branches on the right leading to houses and continue until the path ends at a broad track. Turn right to a road; then right again to the church where this walk started.

Walk 10
HEDGERLEY AND GERRARDS CROSS

This is an undemanding yet attractive route from the centre of one of the prettiest villages in the Chilterns to an exceptional teashop at the heart of a most affluent community. There is one short climb near the start, and then it is downhill or on the level all the way, and there are some pleasing views. Interesting features on the way cover both human and natural history as the route passes through the parkland of one of the several mansions that once surrounded Gerrards Cross and returns past the site the earliest inhabitants chose for their home. It also visits an RSPB reserve on the return leg.

The Tea Tree on Packhorse Road in Gerrards Cross is a traditional and yet innovative tearoom behind a gift shop. It has a most tempting selection of cakes, including, on my visit, an outstanding honey and pecan cake. Other teatime goodies include cream teas with clotted cream, and toasted teacakes or crumpets. For lunch there is a sustaining soup or a choice of salads, such as their own variation on salad nicoise or a warm brie and roasted vegetable salad. There is also a selection of sandwiches and delicious variations on a cheese-on-toast theme, collectively called melts. The daily specials include an irresistible desert. The Tea Tree is open Monday to Saturday between 9 am and 5 pm, with the last orders for cooked food at 4.30 pm. Telephone 01753 882478.

When the teashop is closed the White Horse in Hedgerley at the start of the walk and the Packhorse in Gerrards Cross both serve food.

DISTANCE: 5½ miles.

MAP: OS Explorer 172 Chiltern Hills East, High Wycombe, Maidenhead.

STARTING POINT: The White Horse at Hedgerley (GR 969873).

HOW TO GET THERE: From junction 2 of the M40, take the A355 towards Slough for 2 miles. Turn left along Parish Lane at the Yew Tree on the left, signed 'Hedgerley 1, Stoke Poges 3'. Turn left again at the second crossroads. Drive through the modern village to the old centre beyond and park near the White Horse. There are several spots where a car can be left without causing inconvenience.

ALTERNATIVE STARTING POINT: If you wish to visit the teashop at the beginning or end of your walk, start in Gerrards Cross, where there is ample parking in several car parks near the centre. The most convenient for this walk is the one in Ochrehill Rise (small charge). The teashop is on Packhorse Road, the main street. You will then start the walk at point 11.

THE WALK

Hedgerley is a picture postcard village that takes great pride in itself. It has won the county best-kept village competition several times. This does not concern itself with how pretty a village is but how well it is cared for. Hedgerley, having an attractive array of buildings, and residents who care for it, is a real gem. It was formerly a centre for brick-making, as witnessed by the name of one of the pubs, and there are traces of clay pits round the village. The church is quite modern, having been built in 1852 to replace an earlier one that was demolished. It contains a number of objects from the earlier church, including a piece of 17th century velvet that came from a cloak given by Charles II as an altar cloth.

1. Facing the White Horse, take a surfaced track to the right of the pub and follow it up to the church. At the gates into the churchyard, turn left and follow the path uphill, ignoring a path on the left near the top of the hill. The path eventually joins an unsurfaced track; continue in the same direction to a lane.

2. Turn left for 100 yards; then right along a track. At the end of the track, turn left across the end of a field to a stile and walk ahead a few yards to a road.

3. Turn right over the motorway and continue past Moat Farm.

4. Turn left on a path starting up some steps. Go through a metal kissing gate and ahead to a finger post. At this point the path veers slightly right, shortly to enter a narrow strip of wood and pass a small lake on the left. Be careful not to take a perhaps more obvious path branching right across a field.

5. A green metal fence starts on the right. When this ends, turn right on a fenced path leading to a stile onto a surfaced track.

6. Turn right. Go across the drive to Bulstrode Court and ahead for 30 yards.

Bulstrode Park covers 400 acres and much of it remains unspoilt. The first house was built as the home of the infamous Judge Jeffreys. It passed later to the Duke of Portland and Somerset and, in 1879, was demolished to make way for the present mansion, now used as a conference centre. The Dowager Duchess of Portland, who lived here at the end of the 18th century, was an avid collector. Though she was described by Horace Walpole as 'a simple woman, but perfectly sober and intoxicated only by empty vases', she often entertained King George III and Queen Charlotte, and counted the great and the good of her generation, such as David Garrick and Dr Johnson, among her close friends.

7. Turn left over a stile and follow this most attractive path gently down hill to a kissing gate out of the park.

Tradition has it that the name Bulstrode comes from the exploits of the family who owned this land at the time of the Norman Conquest. William the Conqueror granted the estate to one of his nobles, but the Shobbingtons were not prepared to concede without a fight. They armed their retainers and decided the best form of defence was attack. They charged the enemy camp at night, mounted on bulls. Many of the Normans were killed and the rest fled. When the king heard of this, he gave Shobbington safe passage to London to discuss the matter. The head of the family and his seven sons rode to the

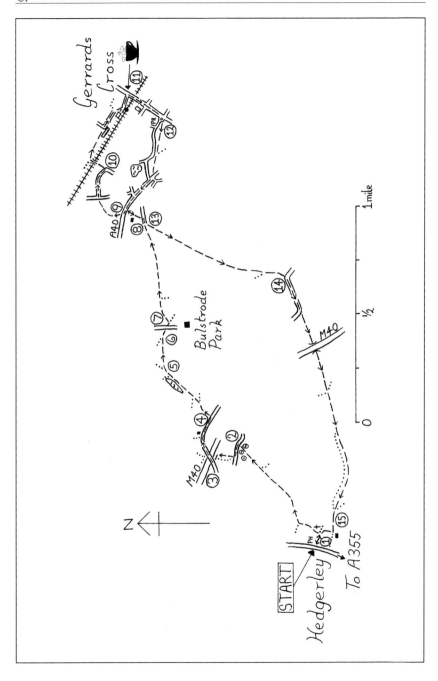

meeting on bulls. Both Shobbington and the king were practical men of the world, and a deal was struck whereby the Shobbingtons could keep their estate if they swore to become William's loyal subjects. They became known as Shobbington Bulstrode and eventually the first name was dropped.

8. Go ahead for 40 yards, past the entrance to Blue Cedars, and then turn left on a signed path to a main road, the A40.

9. Turn left for 30 yards; then right on a signed path. Follow this through to a road and then go ahead along Layters Way.

10. Immediately after Cedar House on the left, turn left on a signed path. Cross the railway and then turn right at a T-junction. Carry on in the same direction along a road, passing Ochrehill Rise car park. When the road ends, bear right down to the station. Turn left up Station Road to the teashop on the opposite side of the main road.

Gerrards Cross takes its name from a local family, Jarrard or Gerrard, and the village grew up round the common at the crossroads. The A40 was the main road between Oxford and London and the Bull was one of the coaching inns along the route. The modern world seemed to have passed it by when the Great Western railway went to the south and the Metropolitan line to the north. Getting to London then involved a coach ride for five dusty miles to Uxbridge; then the Great Western branch line to the main line at West Drayton. All that changed in 1906, when the Great Central railway came and made this attractive spot an extremely desirable – and expensive – place to live, a distinction it retains. A glance in the estate agents' windows will stagger non-residents!

11. Turn left out of the teashop and walk as far as the Packhorse pub on the right.

12. Turn right across the common, roughly parallel with the road beside it, back to the A40. Turn right along the A40 to find the path used earlier. Turn left along it, to the kissing gate into Bulstrode Park.

13. Through the gate, turn left and follow the path through the park to meet a track. Turn left along the track and follow it out of the park to a lane on a bend.

On the hill above you, to the left, is the site of an ancient British encampment, believed to be the largest in Buckinghamshire. Today it is entirely surrounded by exclusive houses and is mainly used by dog walkers, but it once would have dominated the edge of the plateau above the Alderbourne valley and controlled the road below, now the A40.

14. Turn right along the lane, to continue in the same direction. When the lane bends sharp right, continue ahead on a signed path. Follow this through a tunnel under the motorway and press on in the same direction, ignoring several side paths. When a wood starts on the right there is a stile on the right. The public footpath skirts round the outside of the wood, but there is also a parallel path inside the wood, which is an RSPB nature reserve. This path rejoins the right of way further on.

Church Wood is a typical mature mixed wood of oak, ash, and beech. Although there are no particularly unusual species, the reserve has a good range of woodland birds. All three British woodpeckers are found, and you might hear the distinctive noise they make as they tap rapidly at bark to find tasty morsels hidden beneath.

15. Continue in the same direction when the path becomes a track. Just before a house on the left, turn right over a stile and follow the path up to the church. Walk through the churchyard to the surfaced track and follow this back to the start.

Walk 11
PENN AND TYLERS GREEN

*T*his attractive walk is full of historical interest as it explores the area round Penn. It starts at the church, often visited by Americans for its connection with the founding of their country. The route then makes its way by woods, fields and lanes to one of the oldest pubs in England with a fascinating history. A long, gentle climb through woodland brings us to Penn Pond, overlooked by a welcome teashop before the return via Penn Bottom and some fine views of typical Chiltern scenery.

 Florentina is a delightful teashop overlooking Penn Pond, with tables outside in summer to better enjoy this charming spot. In fact, it's properly called Widmer Pond on Tyler's Green but everyone calls it Penn Pond. There is an excellent selection of cakes including carrot cake, lemon drizzle, and rich fruit cake, to be washed down with a range of teas served from capacious pots into an eclectic selection of pretty china cups. The cakes are thoroughly English but the choices for lunch have a more Mediterranean touch, and this is reflected in the light and modern decoration. There is an appetising choice of ciabattina, including cheddar cheese with delicious onion marmalade, corned beef with lemon pickle or mozzarella with pesto. There is also soup in generous bowls and weekly specials such as quiche and lasagne. Perhaps the best day to do this walk would be Thursday when the owner, Laura Sutton, makes a range of tempting desserts for Penn Pudding Club. The choice changes from week to week but includes such favourites as chocolate bread and butter pudding, blackberry and apple pie and tiramisu. In winter Florentina is open every day until 4.30 pm, just closing on Monday afternoon and at 3 pm on Sunday. In summer, the opening hours are extended. Telephone: 01494 819933.

DISTANCE: 4 miles.

MAP: OS Explorer OS Explorer 172 Chiltern Hills East.

STARTING POINT: Holy Trinity church, Penn. GR 915935

HOW TO GET THERE: Penn is on the B474 Hazlemere – Beaconsfield road. Holy Trinity is at the east end of the village and there are some places to park by the church in Pauls Lane.

ALTERNATIVE STARTING POINT: If you wish to visit the teashop at the beginning or end of your walk, start at Penn Pond, where there is some road-side parking. The teashop overlooks the pond. You will then start the walk at point 10.

THE WALK

Penn is a Celtic word meaning 'hill' and the village sits high on the Chilterns overlooking the valley of the River Wye. It was the site of a Roman lookout point, but its defensive position was recognised much earlier and archaeologists have found signs of Bronze and Iron Age activity. It is said that twelve counties can be seen from the top of the church tower. The church seems to have been built of any materials found lying about. As well as the usual flint, the walls contain sarsen stones, Roman bricks, and limestone clunch. It dates back to the 11th century but has been altered many times. The chancel was largely rebuilt in the 18th century. The builders raised the medieval walls, and the different materials can easily be seen. Also note the darker and more regular flint of the 19th century east wall compared to the earlier flint of the rest of the building. There are several interesting features within, including the Penn Doom above the chancel arch. This is a late 15th century painting of Christ in triumph on judgement day, deemed to be the finest of the five such paintings still in existence. At the time of writing it is on loan to the Victoria and Albert museum for an exhibition.

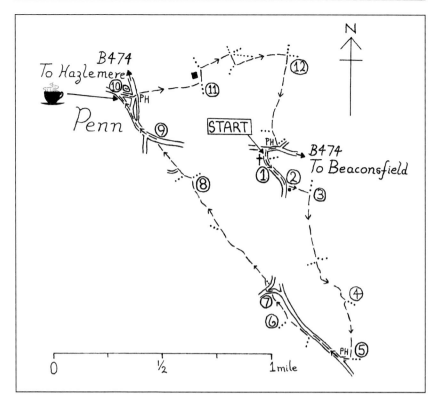

1. With your back to the church, turn right along the lane.

2. Turn left on a signed path immediately before the entrance to Bede House and follow this to a stile and a T-junction with a surfaced drive.

3. Turn right along the drive. When the drive ends continue ahead on a presently unsigned path, ignoring a signed path to the right. Follow the path as it twists and turns through the wood for about ¼ mile.

4. Watch for a post with yellow waymarks and turn right here to a stile out of the wood. Over the stile bear half-left across a field; then continue down the right-hand side of the field and along a hedged path to a track.

5. Turn right, passing the Royal Standard of England, to a lane and turn right along the lane for about 350 yards to a stile on the left. Cross the stile and immediately turn right to continue parallel with the lane. Then follow the path up away from the lane.

The Royal Standard of England is a fascinating old building that has been a pub for many centuries. The story goes that Charles II hid in the roof when he was on the run to France after the Battle of Worcester in 1651. After the Restoration, he showed his gratitude by bestowing the unique name on the inn.

6. Some 15 yards before a stile, turn right to again walk parallel with the lane but now at a higher level to a stile onto a lane.

7. Over the stile turn left along the lane to a junction and at this point turn right on a signed bridleway to shortly reach a T-junction with a wider path. Turn left. Follow this path for a good half mile to a T-junction.

8. Turn left. Ignore a stile on the left and press on uphill, across the end of a lane, to a road.

Penn is the ancestral home of the Penn family. Admiral Penn was highly thought of by Charles II, not only for his loyal service but also because he lent the impoverished king £16,000. William Penn, born in 1644, was his son and the most famous member of the family. He became a Quaker at a time when they were a controversial sect and he was often in trouble with the law. In 1670, he was tried at the Old Bailey for preaching in the streets, the charge being one of conspiring to address and addressing a tumultuous assembly. He pleaded not guilty and disputed the legality of the indictment. Notwithstanding that great pressure was brought to bear upon them, the jury, after a trial lasting four days, acquitted Penn. He, however, went to gaol in default of paying a fine imposed for not removing his hat in court. The jury were also sent to prison.

In 1680, in despair of securing real religious toleration in Europe, Penn began negotiations for the creation of a Quaker settlement in America. Charles II granted him an area of land, perhaps to get rid of this troublesome individual. He called it Sylvania, which was altered at royal command to Pennsylvania, in honour of Penn's father. Penn was named governor of the province and set sail in 1682 to establish a colony where people of all creeds and nationalities could live together in peace. Penn's 'holy experiment' did not go well. His constitution proved unworkable, his principles were flouted, and, from 1692, he was deprived of his powers as governor. Back in London, he lived in poverty in a house chosen for its convenience in escaping by water from his creditors. He died in 1718 and is buried at nearby Jordans.

9. Turn left. When the road forks, bear left to the teashop on the left.

This is Tylers Green. By the 14th century the clay deposits in the area had led to its fame as a centre for producing floor tiles, many of which can still be seen today in Windsor Castle, the Tower of London, and Westminster Palace. Thus the name Tilers (later Tylers) Green emerged.

10. From the teashop cross the road to the green and turn right, passing to the right of Penn Pond to the Red Lion. Take a signed path along a track to the left of the pub. When the track leads through a gate to a house, carry on along a fenced path into a field.

11. Turn left. At the end of the field, turn right to walk along the left-hand side of the field. In the next field turn immediately right. At the bottom of the field, turn left.

12. At a gap in the hedge, turn right uphill on a signed path. Continue ahead when the path leads into a wood, to eventually emerge in a car park. Cross the car park to a road and turn right, back to the start.

Penn always had a reputation as a healthy place. When various plagues affected London in the 15th and 16th centuries, children were often sent to the area to enjoy the fresh air. There was also the first written record at this time of two alehouses – probably the Crown and the Red Lion, both of which are passed on this route. Edmund Burke (see walk 4), the noted parliamentarian, who lived nearby in Beaconsfield, set up a school for the sons of French gentlemen killed in the Revolution. Their caps told of their politics, carrying the message 'Vive le Roi'. The son of a churchwarden was a well-known, not to say infamous, product of Penn. Jack Shrimpton was a notorious highwayman at the start of the 18th century, preying on travellers on the London to Oxford road, near what is now Gerrards Cross. He is reputed to have taken as much as £150 in a day and ended his career on the gallows at Bristol in 1713.

Walk 12
BURNHAM BEECHES AND DORNEY WOOD

Though he knew many of the world's most notable forests, E. H. Wilson, director of the Arnold Arboretum in Harvard, U.S.A., cherished his visit to Burnham Beeches as one of the highlights of his life. An area of natural woodland, bought by the Corporation of London in 1880 as one of the capital's lungs, Burnham Beeches is a National Nature Reserve and a treasure house of wildlife interest. This outstanding walk is definitely one to savour, to take slowly, with your eyes and ears open. It also passes Dorney Wood, a house given to the National Trust for use by a member of the government.

 The Dell lies in a sheltered spot halfway round the route and is open between 10 am and 5 pm every day of the year except Christmas Day. Despite having no indoor accommodation, it is deservedly popular. It offers a good range of cakes, including an exceptional banana cake, as well as a selection of sandwiches and ice creams. Tea is served in capacious mugs rather than pots. Telephone: 01753 646953.

DISTANCE: 4 miles.

MAP: OS Explorer 172 Chiltern Hills East, High Wycombe, Maidenhead.

STARTING POINT: Car park opposite the Blackwood Arms, Common Lane, Littleworth Common (GR 936863).

HOW TO GET THERE: From junction 2 of the M40, take the A355 towards Slough for about ¼ mile. Take the first road on the right, signed 'Littleworth Common 2' for about 1¼ miles. When the road bends right, carry on in the same direction along Abbey Park Lane, signed 'Burnham Beeches'. After about ½ mile, turn right along Boveney Wood Lane, signed 'Burnham 3, Taplow 4' for about ¼ mile. Turn left along Common Lane to a car park on the right, opposite the Blackwood Arms.

ALTERNATIVE STARTING POINT: If you wish to visit the teashop at the beginning or end of your walk, there is a car park opposite The Dell. You will then start the walk at point 7, going up some steps behind The Dell to a drive.

THE WALK

1. Cross the lane and take a signed path over a stile next to a field gate along a track to the right of Woodside Cottage. Follow the clear path across fields and through woods to a lane. Cross the lane and a small car park, and press on in the same direction on a clear track to meet a surfaced drive.

Burnham Beeches is the most important fragment still in existence of the ancient woodland that once covered southern England. We owe a debt of gratitude to the far-sighted naturalist Francis George Heath. It was at his suggestion that the Corporation of the City of London acquired the land as a green lung for the city when Burnham Beeches came on the market, advertised as land suitable for building 'superior residences', in 1879. The Open Spaces Act of 1878 allowed the corporation to buy unenclosed and common land on the edge of London. However, there was a complication: there were two enclosed areas in the middle of the common land. This was solved by the local MP, Sir Henry Peek, who bought the entire lot and then sold the unenclosed parts on to the corporation. Since then, the enclosed areas have been either given to or bought by the corporation, so it now owns the whole of Burnham

Beeches. At the time it was not popular with the local residents who resented the energetic management and flurry of by-laws introduced by the new owners. The first head keeper, Owen Arnett, had a very trying time. More than once angry locals threw him into a pond and on another occasion he was left tied to a tree all night.

2. Turn left and then bear right * after 25 yards, along Halse Drive. Walk along Halse Drive as far as Victoria Drive on the right.

* On the left at the junction, marked by a plaque, is an earthwork variously called Hartley Court, Harlequin's, and Hardicanute's Moat. It consists of an irregular moat surrounding an area of about 1½ acres with a continuous bank on the outside and dividing banks within. The whole is surrounded by a further bank and a ditch, enclosing about 9 acres. Inside the inner moat is evidence of a house and a well. It is thought that the outer area was once cultivated for crops and the inner was the homestead. The banks were probably topped by palisade fencing to protect the cultivated land from deer and pigs grazing in the surrounding woods. The date is uncertain but moated homesteads generally date from the 12th to the 14th centuries.

One condition Sir Henry Peek did insist upon as part of the agreement was that the Corporation of the City of London pay for roads to be built to allow him access to the land he retained, and these roads are named after people involved with the corporation at that time. Most of the drives are now restricted to official vehicles, so they are much more pleasant to walk along.

3. Do not turn right along Victoria Drive but bear slightly right, uphill, on an unsigned path. At the top of the rise, continue ahead, over cross paths and a drive, and downhill to a pond.

4. Turn right, to walk with a stream on your left to a second pond.

These two ponds are not natural but were formed by the damming of a stream in about 1800, and were used for sheep dipping until well into the 19th century. The concrete retaining walls were built during the Second World War by the army, which used the water for washing vehicles. The ponds are particularly attractive in summer, with waterlilies in bloom and colourful dragonflies darting above them. One exotic bird you may spot is the mandarin duck. It was originally from the Far East, but its attractive plumage meant it was highly prized among collectors, and it was

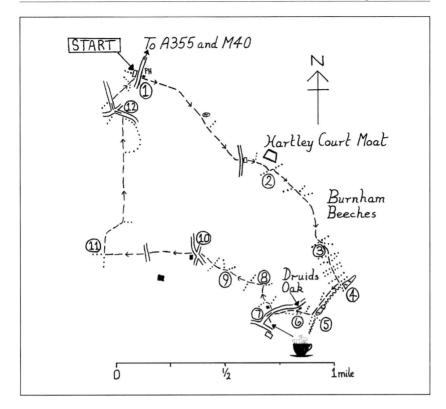

introduced into England in 1745. Inevitably some of the ducks escaped, and found English conditions to their liking. It was accepted as a naturalized breeding bird in 1971 and has been seen here for the last ten years or so. The mandarin is a woodland duck and nests in holes in trees or in the nesting boxes put up for tawny owls. These can be as much as 25 feet off the ground, and the little ducklings leave the nest when they are just a day old!

5. At the far end of the second pond turn right. After about 125 yards, bear right into a clearing, to pass to the left of a venerable tree surrounded by a wooden fence, and walk ahead to a drive.

Burnham Beeches has probably been wooded ever since the forest returned after the last Ice Age. This vestige of ancient woodland contains the largest collection of old beech trees in the world. Nearly all the old beeches have been

71

pollarded, which has contributed to their longevity and given them the weird appearance we see today. A beech tree would ordinarily live for about 250 years, but pollarding allows the tree to live for 400 years or more and grow into the gnarled giants for which Burnham Beeches is famous. There are various stories about how the pollarding started. One says that it was Cromwell's soldiers stationed at Burnham in the winter of 1645, who cut the trees to make musket stocks. Another states that the duchess of Monmouth, who owned a house in Burnham, had the trees lopped as a memorial to her husband, who was executed by James II in 1685. Both of these are romantic nonsense. The practice is an old form of dual-purpose woodland management. The trees have the capacity to sprout new branches and can be cut on a 12 to 15 year rotation. Lopping them at head height keeps the succulent new growth safe from the animals that were allowed to graze the forest floor beneath.

From the middle of the 19th century onwards, the use of wood as a fuel declined as coal became more readily available. There was no longer the same need to harvest a crop from the trees, and pollarding declined. It is thought that at the end of the 18th century there were about 3,000 pollards in Burnham Beeches, but now the number is down to just over 500. Many of the trees have not been cut for nearly 200 years. It is very important to conserve these old trees, as they are a vital habitat for many tiny animals and there are very few places that have as many ancient pollards as Burnham Beeches.

The enclosed tree is thought to be the most ancient in the Beeches. It is fenced to help to protect its roots from the damaging effect of trampling. It is called the Druids Oak, though there is no documented reason for this particular tree having that name; it is probably a bit of Victorian whimsy. Several named trees are marked on old maps but are no longer to be seen. His Majesty was a huge beech pollard that in 1931 had a girth of 28 feet. Sadly, it lost its crown in the severe storms of 1987, though the stump remains. Another was the Maiden Tree, said to be the only major tree in the woods that was not pollarded.

☕ **6.** Turn left beside the drive to the teashop on the left down some steps.

7. Retrace your steps to the drive and turn right for 70 yards. Turn left at a shelter. Go ahead, to walk with a fence on your right. Do not go through the gate into the enclosure.

In the enclosure on the right are the remains of an Iron Age fort dating from the 8th to 5th centuries BC. The site was badly damaged during the Second

World War when the land was fenced off and used by the army for exercises and maintaining vehicles. The camp for personnel was built on top of the fort.

8. At a cross path, turn left downhill. At the bottom of the hill, go over a broad cross track and continue ahead, now uphill.

9. A path joins on the right, and after a further 15 yards the path forks; bear left and follow the path, to emerge at the junction of Park Lane and Green Lane.

10. Go ahead in the same direction across the roads to a signed path to the right of the entrance to a property called Juniper Tree. Follow this across a lane and carry on in the same direction across a field.

The large house glimpsed on the left is Dorney Wood. The house was given to the National Trust as a residence for a minister and is used as the Chancellor of the Exchequer's country retreat. The gardens are opened to the public a couple of weekends a year, to those who make a written application.

11. At the end of the field, the path is enclosed by hedges. Just as the hedges start, turn right on a path waymarked by a yellow arrow on a post, to walk along the right-hand side of three fields. The right of way skirts the right-hand perimeter of a fourth field but in practice goes straight ahead to a stile onto a lane.

12. Turn left for 200 yards over crossroads; then turn right on a signed bridleway that leads through the wood to the car park where this walk started.

This is Littleworth Common. If you look at the trees you will notice that they are very different from those growing in Burnham Beeches; they are much younger and there are far more birches. A hundred years ago the scene would have been far more open, as the trees were prevented from growing by the grazing of the commoners' animals. Open grazing is no longer economic, and, as it declined, the trees invaded. Birch is a fast-growing but short-lived species that swiftly colonizes new opportunities. Come back in another hundred years or so, and, unless grazing is re-established or the trees are managed, there will be more oak and beech. In 300 years it will be indistinguishable from Burnham Beeches.

Walk 13
HURLEY AND MARLOW

This walk is most unusual for the Chilterns, as it is almost completely flat and the only climbing is to cross the bridges over the river. It follows the banks of the Thames, from the ancient village of Hurley, along one of its most interesting – and popular – sections, to Marlow, and there is much to see along the way. The return is by a different and much quieter route, with lovely views of the Chiltern Hills rising behind the flood plain of the river.

 Burgers is a traditional tearoom behind a Swiss patisserie. It has been a family-run business since 1942, when Eric and Marie Burger brought a touch of Switzerland to Buckinghamshire, six years after arriving in England. The cakes are outstanding and with very few exceptions everything is made on the premises. Cream teas comprise Yorkshire blend tea, scones with preserves and cream, and a cake. For lunch there is soup, sandwiches, and various specials or an exceptional Welsh rarebit, made to their own recipe. The tearoom is behind the shop, and you will find it hard to resist the exquisite chocolates. At

Christmas there are wonderful Christmas cakes and puddings and at Easter their famous chocolate eggs. Burgers is open every day except Sunday until 5.30 pm. Telephone: 01628 483389.

If you choose to do this walk on a Sunday, there are several other places of refreshment in Marlow on or near the High Street.

An alternative (or additional!) tea stop is the lock keeper's cottage at Temple Lock, beautifully situated on an island. Teas are served in the garden at weekends from Easter onwards and during the school summer holidays. This is just the place to idle away an hour on a sunny afternoon, overlooking a lovely stretch of the river with the traffic through the lock to watch. A small selection of delicious cakes is available, with cookies or ice cream as alternatives. The opening hours are flexible, depending rather on the weather, since there is no indoor accommodation, but teas are generally served in summer from 11 am until 5.30 pm. Telephone: 01628 824333.

DISTANCE: 5½ miles.

MAP: OS Explorer 172 Chiltern Hills East, High Wycombe, Maidenhead.

STARTING POINT: Hurley car park (GR 826840).

HOW TO GET THERE: From the A4130, Henley–Burchetts Green road, 4 miles east of Henley, take a signed road into Hurley village. This is the High Street. After ½ mile, bear left to a car park at the end of the road near the church.

ALTERNATIVE STARTING POINT: If you wish to visit the teashop at the beginning or end of your walk, start in Marlow, where there is ample parking in the car park in Pound Lane (charge). The teashop is on the High Street, opposite the junction with Pound Lane. You will then start the walk at point 5.

THE WALK

Hurley is a very ancient village that grew up at an important ford across the Thames. The first church, built about 700 AD, may have suffered at the hands of the marauding Danes. After the Norman Conquest, William I confiscated all the land and gave it to his trusted supporter Geoffrey de Mandeville. He built a priory here, which became very wealthy over the following centuries, and there are still many remains. After the Dissolution of the Monasteries, the Lovelace family acquired the priory estate for £1,500 in 1545. There is an elaborate monument to them in the church. Much of the material from the priory was used to build a mansion, Ladye Place. Before this, the church was much bigger than it is now. The church is well worth exploring and has a guidebook available, which also covers the priory remains.

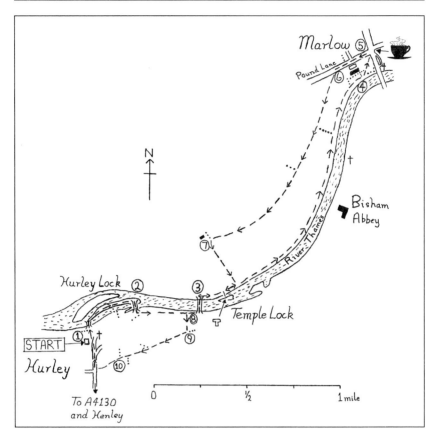

1. Return to the car park entrance and turn left on a public footpath. Cross the river bridge; turn right past Hurley Lock to the next bridge.

2. Recross the river and turn left along the riverside path to the next bridge.

3. Cross the river yet again and turn right. Follow the riverside path to Marlow.

Across the river is Bisham Abbey. It once belonged to the Knights Templar and today it is a national sports centre. The present building is mainly Tudor and was built by Henry VIII. For many years it belonged to the Hoby family, and it is said to be haunted by the ghost of one Lady Hoby. She punished her little boy for untidiness in his copybook by locking him in a cupboard. Later that day she was called away to another part of the country, and forgot to release her son or tell anyone where he was. By the time she returned, he had starved to death in the cupboard. It is said that some 16th century copybooks were found during restoration work.

4. As you come into Marlow, the riverside path is in a park. This is Higginson Park, given to the people of Marlow. Level with a building on the left (Court Gardens), bear left away from the river to emerge from the park at the bottom of the High Street. The teashop is just across the road.

Marlow is an ancient and prosperous town, with many Georgian buildings hidden behind modern shop fronts, and well worth taking the time to explore. Marlow can also claim more Olympic gold medals than many countries, thanks to the efforts of its most famous son, the rower Steve Redgrave, who started his career at Great Marlow School.

5. From the teashop, cross the High Street and walk along Pound Lane.

6. Bear left along a track called Lower Pound Lane and continue for about a mile to a T-junction by a house.

7. Turn left on a surfaced track that leads back to the river. Turn right along the riverside path by the Thames. Cross Temple Bridge to the other bank and turn right for 125 yards.

8. Turn left on a signed path.

9. At a T-junction, turn right on a track. Ignore both the path on the right into a caravan site and a track on the left.

10. As the track bends right, turn left on a fenced path to continue in the same direction into Hurley. Turn right through the village, back to the car park.

Walk 14
HAMBLEDON AND HENLEY

This route goes from a charming and historic Chiltern village along one of the most famous stretches of the River Thames – the regatta course – to Henley. The return route lies over the hills on the south side of the river and has some excellent views of typical Chiltern scenery. It also visits the picture postcard Hambleden Lock and Mill.

The menu at Crispins, by the bridge in Henley-on-Thames, features a selection of set teas, such as chocolate cake tea, meringue glacé tea, and cream tea. For lunch there is a wide choice, including snacks such as chicken terrine or ploughman's and full meals, both hot and cold. It is an attractive traditional teashop with a cheerful, friendly atmosphere enhanced by a pleasant background of light classical music. It is open every day except Monday (open Bank Holiday Mondays) until about 8.30 pm. During the week it opens at noon and at the weekends at 10 am. Telephone: 01491 574232.

When this teashop is closed there are several others, as well as restaurants and pubs, in Henley-on-Thames. The route also passes the Stag and Huntsman pub in Hambleden and the Flowerpot at Aston, which is very popular, although hidden away.

DISTANCE: 6 miles.

MAP: OS Explorer 171 Chiltern Hills West, Henley-on-Thames & Wallingford.

STARTING POINT: Public car park in Hambleden next to the Stag and Huntsman (GR 785866).

HOW TO GET THERE: At Mill End, 3 miles from Henley or 5 miles from Marlow on the A4155, Henley–Marlow road, turn up the road signed 'Hambleden, Skirmett and Fingest'. Turn right into Hambleden village on a road signed 'Pheasant's Hill 1 Frieth 3 Lane End 4'. In the centre of the village, when the main road bends left, continue ahead past the Stag and Huntsman to a car park on the right.

ALTERNATIVE STARTING POINT: If you wish to visit the teashop at the beginning or end of your walk, start in Henley. where there are several signed car parks. The teashop is across the road from the bridge across the river Thames. You will then start the walk at point 8.

THE WALK

1. Walk back through the village to the road you were on before turning into Hambleden, ignoring a footpath by a bridge.

Hambleden is a picturesque village with a remarkable amount of history for such a small place. The church of St Mary is worth a visit, even by those not usually interested in such things. It was first built in Saxon times but the font is probably the only survivor from that date. The structure we see today is Norman, though there has been much rebuilding and restoring down the ages. The Norman tower collapsed in 1703, and the present one was built 18 years later. The monuments include one to Sir Cope D'Oyley, his wife, and their ten children. Some children are shown holding skulls: sadly, these children died before their parents. The inscription detailing the virtues of Lady D'Oyley is said to be by her brother, the Poet Laureate Francis Quarles, and is particularly fine, though too long to quote here. The oak altar in the south transept is an excellent example of early 16th century carving, and includes the arms of Cardinal Wolsey and Bishop Fox. The panelling was once a bed head, believed to belong to the Sandys family of The Vyne, where Wolsey was a frequent visitor. It came to Hambleden through the marriage of a member of the family to a Scrope, long-time lords of the manor.

Hambleden has three famous sons. Thomas de Cantilupe was the Chancellor of England and Bishop of Hereford. He was the last pre-reformation English saint and was born at the manor house in 1218. The church used to contain some of his relics. Adrian Scrope, who was one of the signatories of the death warrant of Charles I, came from Hambleden, as did Lord Cardigan, who led the Light Brigade into the 'Valley of Death'. A famous adopted son was W.H. Smith, the stationer, who was satirised by Gilbert and Sullivan in HMS Pinafore because 'he never went to sea and rose to be Ruler of the Queen's Navee'. He is buried in the churchyard and shares his resting place with Major George Howson, who started the tradition of wearing poppies on Armistice Day.

In 1315, Hambleden was granted a charter from Edward II to hold a fair. It was revived in 1955 to raise money for the church and school. It was held on Midsummer's Eve but was discontinued after a few years because of rowdy behaviour.

2. Cross the road and take a public footpath opposite. Ignore branches to the left and continue uphill. Just over the brow of the hill, ignore a path on the right and continue ahead, downhill.

3. At a T-junction turn right for 5 yards and then left on a path leading to a wooden gate into a field. Follow the path down the left-hand side of the field, across a stile, and across a second field to a stile onto a farm track. Cross the track to yet another stile and press ahead to a main road.

4. Turn right along the road for quarter of a mile.

5. Turn left over a stile and follow the signed path to the bank of the Thames, crossing the drive to Henley Management College and footbridges over streams.

6. Turn right onto the path along the bank of the Thames and follow it for a mile, passing under an arch.

The stately home passed on the right is Fawley Court, now a Catholic college. The island at the point where you reached the river, Temple Island, is now owned by the Stewards of Henley regatta. It has a white 'temple' built in 1771 as a vista for Fawley Court and is the start of the 1 mile 550 yards long regatta course.

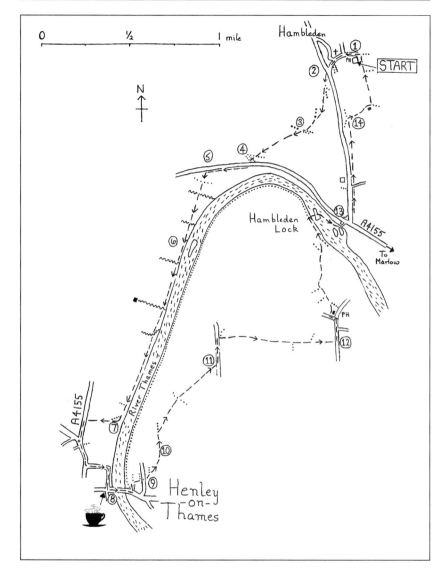

For more than 150 years, Henley has been synonymous with rowing. The first regatta took place on 14th June 1839, with four races held between 4 pm and 7 pm. It has now grown to five days of racing, held in the first week of July, with over 350 entries from all over the world. The Royal part of its title originated in 1861, when Prince Albert became its patron. The total cost of *staging the five-day regatta is now nearly £1.7 million a year. About 75% of this comes from subscriptions paid by members of the Stewards' Enclosure, for which there is always a long waiting list, and their purchases of additional badges for their guests. The regatta is one of the few major sporting occasions today that operates without any reliance upon commercial sponsorship or outside subsidy. The regatta owns the land on the opposite bank where the enclosures and car parks are situated and some of the land on this bank. To preserve the natural beauty of the Henley reach of the Thames, every part of the regatta's installations, both on land and in the river, is removed each year and then re-erected the following year so that there is no trace of the regatta between September and March.*

7. When the path along the riverbank ends at a fence, go through a metal kissing gate on the right and follow the path up to the road. Turn left and then bear left at the roundabout along the main road into Henley. Turn left along New Road, towards the river, and turn right beside the river. The teashop is on the crossroads by the bridge.

On the left on New Street is the Kenton Theatre, originally built in 1805 by two actor-managers named Penley and Jonas. From 1813 the building became a non-conformist chapel, a Church of England school, an empty shell, a church hall, and a scenery store. Then, in 1935, it opened again as a theatre and, despite a sometimes precarious existence, it has managed to remain so ever since. Also on New Street was Brakspear's Brewery. Local beer drinkers were angry and disappointed when the name was sold to a national brewer and the site acquired by a hotel chain.

8. Turn right out of the teashop and cross the bridge. Some 50 yards beyond the far side of the bridge, turn left. Ignore the Thames Path bearing left almost immediately and go ahead for 80 yards and through double metal gates. Turn right to a gap in the hedge to the right of another set of metal gates. Cross a lane and continue in the same direction on a signed public footpath.

9. At the far side of the field do not take the obvious track on the left but go over a stile and bear half-left towards a wood. As you enter the wood, look on the ground on the left for the memorial to Minty, a much loved dog.

10. Cross a stile and follow the path gently uphill. When a wooden fence starts on the left, bear right to a stile into a wood. Follow the path through the wood. On leaving the wood, cross a permitted path and bear half-right on a gently rising path.

11. At a lane, turn left for 250 yards. Turn right over a stile by metal gates. Follow the track ahead. When the track bends left, continue in the same direction on a signed footpath to a lane.

12. Turn left to The Flowerpot hotel. Turn left along Remenham Lane; then right in just over 50 yards on a signed path along a surfaced track. Follow this to the river. Cross the river at the lock and follow the path across the weir and to a road.

Hambleden Lock with its white, weather-boarded mill is very picturesque and much photographed. There has been a lock here since the 14th century, and a mill dating back to 1388. The present building is 16th century and was working until 1958. It is now converted into flats.

13. Turn right and then left after 35 yards, along a road signed 'Hambleden, Skirmett and Fingest'. After ¼ mile there is a lane on the right. Take a signed public footpath into a field at this point. Follow the path parallel with the road towards Hambleden.

In 1812 the remains of a Roman farmstead were excavated in a field just by the car park on the left. The finds used to be kept in a small museum in Hambleden but have now been removed to a museum in Aylesbury, where they are displayed together with photographs of the site.

14. At the end of the field, turn right along a cross track. Some 50 yards after a barn, turn left on a track. This ends at a drive. Turn left for a few yards back to the car park.

Walk 15
SHIPLAKE

This undemanding stroll explores the countryside round the Thames-side community of Shiplake. It is very varied, with an attractive stretch by the river, as well as woodland and field paths, and some good views.

 The Wildlife Café at Wyevale Garden Centre on Reading Road, near Henley-on-Thames is in an airy glass building (previously a greenhouse, one suspects). It sustains the theme with murals of animals, a cane-lined roof, and rattan furniture. Several tables outside overlook the displays of plants. There is a good selection of cakes and other teatime favourites, including cream teas with delicious scones and clotted cream. For a light lunch, sandwiches, crusty baguettes, or jacket potatoes with a range of fillings are available. There is also a tempting choice of daily specials, such as stuffed peppers or Welsh rarebit. A warming alternative to tea on a cold winter day is hot chocolate with cream and chocolate flake and/or marshmallows. The teashop is open every day throughout the year, between 9.30 am and

5 pm on Monday to Saturday and 10.30 am to 4 pm on Sunday. Telephone: 0118 9403865.

DISTANCE: 4 miles.

MAP: OS Explorer 171 Chiltern Hills West, Henley-on-Thames & Wallingford.

STARTING POINT: Shiplake station car park (GR 776797).

HOW TO GET THERE: In Lower Shiplake, on the A4155, Henley-on-Thames–Caversham road, about 2 miles south of Henley, turn along Station Road. Follow this to the station car park on the right.

ALTERNATIVE STARTING POINT: If you wish to visit the teashop at the beginning or end of your walk, start at Wyevale Garden Centre on the A4155, about 1½ miles south of Henley, where there is a large car park. The teashop is in the garden centre. Permission should be sought before leaving a car for a lengthy period. You will then start the walk at point 9, turning right out of the garden centre.

THE WALK

The railway came to the parish of Shiplake in 1858 and passed through the hamlet of Lashbrook, about a mile from the old village. The attraction of easy commuting caused the centre of the community to shift about a mile northeast.

1. Return to the road and turn left, past the Baskerville Arms. Turn left along Mill Road for about ½ mile.

2. Opposite Crowsley Road, turn left along the drive to Lashbrook Farm for 50 yards; then turn right down three steps and over a stile, signed 'Shiplake Lock ¼'. Follow the path to a lane. Turn right for 25 yards; then left, signed 'Sonning 3' to Shiplake Lock.

3. Turn right to walk with the Thames on the left.

The brick building ahead, in a beautiful position on a bluff overlooking the river, is Shiplake Court. The old house was demolished in 1804, after the owner had gambled away all his money and the house fell into disrepair. It was rebuilt in 1894 and is now a boys' public school.

4. At Shiplake College boathouse, bear right, away from the river, on a path that starts between boathouses and is waymarked with a blue arrow on a post. At a T-junction with a track, do not turn along the track but take the waymarked path sharp right up to Shiplake church.

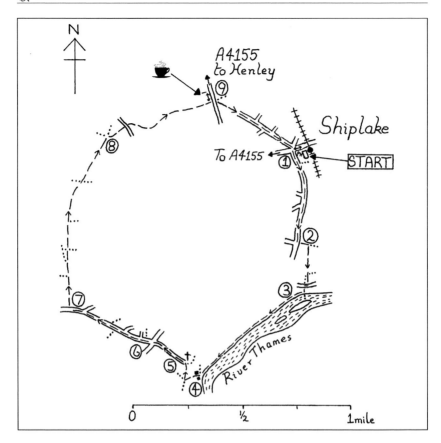

This is the original village of Shiplake. During the first half of the 19th century, the estate fell on hard times and there was almost no building, which is why the old village isn't more substantial. There has been a church here for more than 1,000 years and there is information available within about its interesting features. Its modern claim to fame is that this is where the poet Tennyson married Emily Sellwood. He was a friend of the vicar, and Emily was a cousin of the vicar's wife. They had known each other for many years, but Emily's father opposed the match, poetry being a precarious living. In 1850 Tennyson's luck changed. His poem, In Memoriam, was published and made his name besides bringing sufficient income for him to marry Emily. A few weeks later he was appointed Poet Laureate and his position was assured.

5. Turn left along a lane to a main road.

6. Cross the road and walk along Plough Lane opposite for about ½ mile.

7. Some 150 yards after Memorial Avenue, turn right along a tree-lined track, Kiln Lane. When the main track bends left, continue ahead along a footpath along a smaller track. When this track in turn bears left, continue ahead and follow the path into Hailey Wood. Ignore all side paths and follow the main path through the wood and on across a field to a surfaced drive.

8. Turn right. Cross a lane and carry on along the track, signed 'Lower Shiplake ¾'. At a main road, turn left for 80 yards to the entrance to the garden centre and the teashop.

9. Retrace your steps to the junction of the track and the road. Cross the road and go over a stile to the right of a track giving onto a fenced path. When the path ends, continue in the same direction along a road to the Baskerville Arms. Turn left, back to the car park where this walk started. (If you started at the teashop, cross the road at the Baskerville Arms and continue ahead along Mill Lane.)

Shiplake Lock

Walk 16
BIX AND GREYS COURT

This is an outstanding walk in Chiltern woods that I return to time and time again. Enjoyable at all times of year, it is at its incomparable best in early May when the woodland floor mirrors the sky and the air is heavy with the scent of bluebells.

I do not usually recommend walks where you have to pay to access the tearoom, but this walk is so good that I am making an exception. Greys Court is a National Trust property, and you have to pay the entrance fee to visit the tearoom unless you are a member of the National Trust. And this means you can combine tea with a visit to the lovely gardens and interesting features of the property. The tearoom is housed in the 16th century Cromwellian stables, and there are a couple of tables outside as well. The building has been put to many uses down the centuries. The name comes from its use as a stables and mess room by Parliamentary troops during the Civil War. The unusual and attractive modern furniture highlights the antiquity of the room. There is an excellent selection of cakes and other teatime favourites, including satisfyingly gooey flapjacks. The tearoom at Greys Court is open from April to September, from Tuesday to Saturday and Bank Holiday Mondays, between 2.15 pm and 5.15 pm. It is also open on Wednesdays in March and October. Telephone 01491 628529.

When the teashop is closed, or for a lunch stop, the Dog and Duck at Highmoor is well known for its excellent food (including a most substantial ramblers' repast) and pleasant garden. Telephone 01491 641261.

DISTANCE: 5½ miles.

MAP: OS Explorer 171 Chiltern Hills West, Henley-on-Thames & Wallingford.

STARTING POINT: St James's church, Bix (GR 728854).

HOW TO GET THERE: From the A4130, Henley–Nettlebed road, about 3 miles northwest of Henley, take a minor road signed 'Bix Village' to a parking area to the right of the church.

ALTERNATIVE STARTING POINT: If you wish to visit the teashop at the beginning or end of your walk, start at Greys Court, where there is ample parking. The teashop is in Greys Court (charge unless you are a member of the National Trust). You will then start the walk at point 9.

THE WALK

The unusual name of Bix is thought to derive from the Old English word byxe, meaning 'box tree', possibly 'box wood'. The church is relatively modern, built in the last quarter of the 19th century. The old church of St James lies a mile from the village and was abandoned in 1875 when the keystone fell from the chancel arch.

1. With your back to the entrance to the church, turn right across a road to take a signed footpath to the left of a phone box. This leads shortly to the main road. Turn right along the footway for just under 300 yards.

2. At the end of the dual carriageway, turn left along a track signed 'Right of Way'. When the main track bends left as the drive to Bromsden Farm, continue ahead for nearly a mile, ignoring a track on the left. Press on along the main track as it bends left and goes uphill. Bear right, still on the main track, at the next junction.

3. Shortly after passing a large house on the left, turn left along a track. Continue ahead over a surfaced drive to the road and the Dog and Duck.

4. Turn left along the road for 125 yards, noticing the topiary on the right, and then left along a signed path along a track. Bear left after 30 yards; then turn left after a further 30 yards. Follow the path through the woods, guided by the occasional yellow arrows on trees, to meet a major cross path. Press on ahead to eventually reach a stile out of the wood.

5. Over the stile, bear right, crossing a surfaced drive and passing to the right of a copse, to find another stile back into woodland. Follow the path ahead to a cross path; this can be muddy and there is a parallel path to the right that rejoins the main path.

6. Turn right for about 400 yards. At a major cross path, bear left over a stile onto a signed, more or less parallel National Trust walkers' path and continue in the same direction.

7. Within sight of a stile and gate onto a lane, bear left, slightly uphill, to reach a surfaced drive. (If you arrive at the lane, you have gone 35 yards too far.)

8. Turn left. Walk along the drive past Greys Court to the entrance kiosk; then retrace your steps along the drive to the pedestrian entrance.

Mary Russell Mitford described Greys Court as 'framed like a picture by the rarest and stateliest of trees and erected amongst the remains of a vast old castellated mansion....' in her book Recollections of a Literary Life. *This is still a good description of Greys, despite having being written in 1851. You are taken back through centuries of building, from times of great wealth and pleasure to more dangerous times when castellated towers and walls were built to make the life of those within more secure. At the time of* Domesday Book *a branch of the de Grey family owned the Rotherfield estate. They were a powerful and influential lot, who served the Crown in many capacities, mainly military. There seems hardly to have been a battle from Edward I's conquest of Wales, through the campaigns against William Wallace in Scotland, to the*

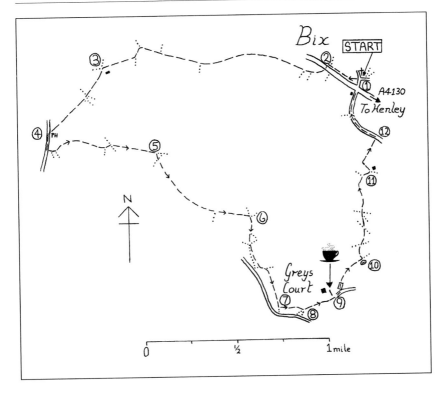

Hundred Years' War in which a de Grey was not prominent. In those days you could not just build a castle. Licence to crenellate was granted to John de Grey, second Baron Grey of Rotherfield, after his service at the Battle of Crecy in 1346. The line died out after the Battle of Bosworth, when the last member of the family presumably died; his fate remained a mystery. The estate then passed to the Knollys family, who built their Elizabethan mansion within the defence.

During the reign of James I, Greys Court was involved in one of the greatest scandals of the age. One Frances Howard was the then owner's sister-in-law. She divorced her husband, the Earl of Essex, and planned to marry Robert Carr, the heir to the Earl of Somerset. Sir Thomas Overbury, a friend and adviser to Carr, opposed the marriage, but Frances managed to get him sent to the Tower. He died while he was incarcerated, and Frances confessed to having been instrumental in having poison mixed into his food. Her husband protested his innocence but both were convicted. They were initially imprisoned in the Tower but then pardoned and banished into confinement at Greys Court.

In 1937 Sir Felix and Lady Brunner bought the estate and created the fine

91

gardens and walks around Greys that can be enjoyed today. In 1969 they gave it to the National Trust.

9. After exploring Greys Court, retrace your steps to the drive and entrance kiosk. Immediately after the kiosk, bear left off the drive through a field used as a car park to a stile. Over the stile, carry on along the left-hand side of two fields.

10. Some 40 yards after crossing a bridge over a marshy area beside a pond, bear left up some steps and through a small gate. Follow the path through the woods; then on across two fields to a surfaced drive. Cross the drive and bear half-left across a third field to a stile back into woodland. Go over a cross path after a few yards and press on ahead through the woods. Watch out for a half-timbered house out of the woods to the right.

11. Level with the house, turn right through a small gate out of the woods, and walk along the right-hand side of a small field to a track by the house. Turn left.

12. At a lane, turn left again and follow this to the main road. Cross the road and carry on along the lane into Bix and the starting point.

Just before the main road on the left is Bix water tank. Water supplies have always been a problem throughout the Chilterns. This brick-lined pond was built at the end of the 19th century to supply water for steam-powered vehicles on the Oxford road out of Henley and agricultural machinery. It was in use until the 1940s but then fell into dereliction. It was recognized in 1998 and has been restored. A plaque tells you more of its history and present management.

Walk 17
GORING

At Goring Gap the mighty Thames breaks through the chalk hills of southern England. It was an important river crossing from time immemorial and is now guarded by the twin towns of Goring and Streatley. The gap is usually taken as the southwestern limit of the Chilterns, and this walk explores that corner of the Area of Outstanding Natural Beauty. It is a pleasant mixture of fields and woods, with a not too challenging climb giving some extensive views to the Downs across the river. This is followed by a stretch along one of the most beautiful reaches of the river Thames before tea in Goring completes an enjoyable expedition.

 The Riverside is, as the name implies, very close to the Thames in Goring. It has a pleasant, airy atmosphere and there are tables outside, both at the front and in the pleasant garden at the back. It is an unusual establishment because it has a completely split personality.

During the day it is a very traditional teashop, serving a variety of cakes, as well as the usual scones and teacakes. For lunch, a wide selection of sandwiches and full meals are served, and the only hint of its other personality is the vegetable samosas on the menu. It is open from 10 am until 4.30 pm, every day except Monday, throughout the year. By night it becomes an Indian restaurant – an unusual arrangement, but it seems to work. Telephone: 01491 872243.

When the teashop is closed there are several pubs in Goring that serve food.

DISTANCE: 4½ miles.
MAP: OS Explorer 171 Chiltern Hills West, Henley-on-Thames & Wallingford.
STARTING POINT: Goring station car park (GR 603805).
HOW TO GET THERE: If you approach the town from the east, the station car park is signed to the left from the B4526 on the outskirts of Goring
ALTERNATIVE STARTING POINT: If you wish to visit the teashop at the beginning or end of your walk, start in Goring where there is some parking in Manor Road, signed from the main road through the village. The teashop is on the main road to the right. You will then start the walk at point 9.

THE WALK

1. With your back to the station, return left along the road. Turn right at the Queen's Arms. Take the second road on the right, Whitehills Green. Follow the road round to the left, and then right, to find a path between hedges leading to a stile onto a playing field.

2. Cross to the far left corner of the playing field to pick up a clear path along the left-hand side of two fields.

3. At the end of the second field, follow the boundary downhill to the right, to a stile into a wood. Follow the clear path uphill through the wood for about ½ mile to a broad cross path and then continue ahead for a further 100 yards.

4. Turn right, uphill, on a path waymarked with yellow arrows on a tree at the time of writing. Continue ahead at an oblique cross path. As you approach the end of the wood, bear right at a fork; then left after a couple of yards to a stile out of the wood. Keep ahead across a field towards farm buildings to a stile onto a track.

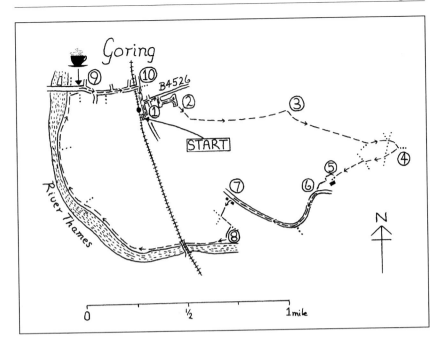

5. Turn right. Immediately before a gate into the first field, turn left to find a stile onto an extremely narrow, fenced path. Fortunately, there are only a few yards of this before another stile into a small field. Cross this diagonally to another stile and on to a further stile onto a lane.

6. Turn right. Walk along the lane for about ½ mile, following it round a right-hand bend.

7. Turn left on a track between cottages. At a concrete cross track, turn left for 135 yards; then turn right, signed 'Thames path', to the river.

There are many swans living on the Thames. The Royal Swan Upping takes place every year in late July. It starts at Sunbury Lock and ends at Abingdon Bridge. The ceremony dates from medieval times, when the Crown claimed ownership of all mute swans, which were an important food source in those days. Ownership has been shared with the Vintners' and Dyers' Livery Companies since the 15th century. The Queen's Swan Marker, accompanied by the Swan Uppers of the Vintners' and Dyers' companies, uses six traditional Thames rowing skiffs in their five-day journey upstream. The Queen's Swan

Marker and the Swan Uppers wear scarlet uniforms, and each boat flies appropriate flags and pennants. The swans are counted and the cygnets weighed and measured, and all are checked for any sign of injury. Dates and approximate times at locks are available from the Office of The Queen's Swan Marker. Phone 01628 523030.

☕ **8.** Follow the path to the right, upriver, under a railway bridge, and continue to Goring. Turn right immediately before a road bridge and follow the path to the road and teashop on the other side.

Goring, like the other Thames-side towns of Henley (walk 13, page 80) and Marlow (walk 12, page 77) visited on the walks in this book, is an ancient settlement. Streatley is its twin across the river, and in modern times, with the bridge, they are one place. At one time the two towns were linked by a ferry and a ford. In 1674 a ferry capsized and all 60 people on board were drowned. On the other hand, Goring seems good for your health. In the church is a memorial to one Hugh Whistler, who died in 1615 aged 216!

9. Turn left out of the teashop and walk up through Goring and across the railway.

The Miller of Mansfield inn is a mixture of three buildings – a 17th century brick and flint wing, a Georgian main block, and Victorian additions. It is a very popular resting place with people walking the Ridgeway, which crosses the Thames here. The name is supposed to derive from an early innkeeper, who came from Sherwood Forest. King Henry II was out hunting and became separated from his party. He begged a bed and meal from a miller, who had no idea of his guest's identity. His wife served what she called a 'lightfoot pastry' and the king remarked that it tasted like venison, which of course it couldn't be, since all deer belonged to the king and poaching them was such a serious offence. The miller said that what the king didn't know wouldn't harm him and that he had several carcases in the roof. The next day the rest of the hunting party found the king, and the miller saw the noose beckon. However, the king was so grateful for the miller's generosity that he let him off providing he continued to provide hospitality to weary travellers. It makes a good story, anyway!

10. At a T-junction, turn right, back to the car park where this walk started. (If you started in Goring turn left at the Queen's Head.)